DATE DUE			

WITHDRAWN

RESPONDING TO CRIME

CRIMINAL CAREERS

Volume One
EXPLAINING CRIMINALS

Volume Two
KILLING ONE ANOTHER

Volume Three
LYING, CHEATING, STEALING

Volume Four
RESPONDING TO CRIME

RESPONDING TO CRIME

GWYNN NETTLER

Professor Emeritus of Sociology
University of Alberta
Edmonton, Canada

CRIMINAL CAREERS VOLUME FOUR

Anderson Publishing Co. / Cincinnati, Ohio

Rick Adams, Publisher's Staff Editor

CRIMINAL CAREERS VOLUME FOUR: RESPONDING TO CRIME

Library of Congress Cataloging in Publication Data
Nettler, Gwynn.
    Responding to crime.

    (Criminal careers ; v. 4)
    Bibliography: p.
    Includes indexes.
    1. Criminal justice, Administration of. I. Title
II. Series: Nettler, Gwynn. Criminal careers ; v. 4.
HV7431.N47   364   81-70994
ISBN 0-87084-603-5   AACR2

Designed by William A. Burden

Criminal Justice Studies
Anderson Publishing Co./Cincinnati, Ohio

John L. Mason, President   Jean C. Martin, Executive Editor

CONTENTS OF CRIMINAL CAREERS

DETAILED ANALYSIS OF VOLUME FOUR

PREFACE

One way to study social behavior is to think about the courses of lives. All thoughtful people engage in this work, formally or informally. Journalists, novelists and social scientists are vocationally dedicated to this task, but others who do not chart careers for a living also have opinions about what produces kinds of careers. Such opinions affect the guidance of one's own life and influence choices among public policies.

Professional students of social life have attended to segments of people's careers. These segments include childhoods, educational paths, marriages in happiness and misery, occupational shifts and continuities, and health and longevity.

The present work is in the tradition of such studies, but it attends to certain crimes as major nodes or characteristics of careers. However, the principles that inform our study have general applicability. These principles, tentatively formulated, can be applied to the interpretation of any style of life—criminal or lawful, successful, failed, or in-between. These themes provide, then, an introduction to the study of social behavior. An introduction is not a completion, of course, and our study is justified if it describes the difficulties of observing human action and of explaining it.

The text is divided into four volumes. The first part of Volume One (*Explaining Criminals*) describes interpretive themes. These are prescriptions for thinking about careers, criminal or lawful. These themes constitute assumptions that run like a thread through the substantive chapters on kinds of crime (Volumes Two, *Killing One Another*, and Three, *Lying, Cheating, Stealing*) and on modes of responding to crime (Volume Four, *Responding to Crime*).

The second half of Volume One develops these themes by outlining major causes of conduct. These chapters show that human action is not spun out of a simple string of causes, as it is popular to assume. On the contrary, careers are produced in a dense web of influences. A conclusion that follows is that we can know something about what the causes of conduct *can be* without knowing what they *will be* for particular individuals and particular acts.

Volume Two describes homicidal occasions. Attention is addressed to description on both aggregate and individual levels. It is emphasized that description is part of scientific explanation, but that it is not the whole of such explanation, and that there is but little science in the study of conduct.

Volume Three applies our interpretive themes in description of varieties of dishonesty, and Volume Four discusses modes of responding to crime and their justifications.

This work is intended for students of criminology, deviance, and criminal justice. It also' has relevance to studies of the relations between information, knowledge, and private and public policy.

Instructors in departments of psychology and sociology, and in schools of law, criminal justice, and social work may use one volume, or all, and in any order. However, this is a book that tells a story. It reads best from beginning to end.

A booklet of discussion and test questions for each volume is available as a teaching aid. In addition, each chapter begins with an abstract that provides a study and lecture outline.

ACKNOWLEDGEMENTS

William R. Avison, Rollin C. Dudley, James C. Hackler, and Robert A. Silverman read portions of this manuscript and I thank them, and anonymous reviewers, for their suggestions. None of these readers is to blame, of course, for any of my continuing errors.

Jennefer Fraser worked with me for two years as a "detective of data." I am particularly grateful to her for her diligence and enthusiasm. I wish also to thank the editor of these volumes, Rick Adams, for his attention, imagination, and editorial advice.

Gwynn Nettler

1 DOING JUSTICE

Abstract • Response to crime is justified by appeal to two tangled standards: That of right action and that of correct action. ○ Morality sets limits to efficiency. ○ Conflicts persist between what we say we want to achieve, what we are willing to do, and what we do. ○ The "paradox of social choice" applies to response to crime. Multiple objectives, differentially ranked by a diverse population, preclude formation of a completely rational social policy. Compromise results. • Responses to crime are justified by two overlapping objectives: To do justice and to protect society. • Demand for justice is a moral demand. ○ This means that the ends of justice are ultimates, not instruments. ○ Moral prescriptions/proscriptions are not to be confused with practical recommendations. ○ To "know what one is doing" is to be able to tell the difference between acting efficiently and acting morally. ○ The quality of justice is shown to be relative to time, place, and people. • Demand for justice includes demand for arrest, reprobation, retribution, restitution, and fair application of the criminal law. This chapter discusses the first four demands. Chapter 2 discusses justice in administration of the law. • To arrest means to stop. ○ Arresting is sometimes deterrent. ○ Stopping is also sometimes therapeutic. • Reprobation is condemnation. Condemnation is a consequence of moral training. ○ Moral mandates are distinguished from practical assessments. ○ Moral codes claim "superiority" and "legitimacy." These ideas are described. ○ A moral demand is, for its advocates, an ultimate, not an instrument. • Retribution is a common quality of justice. It asks that wrongs not go unpunished. ○ Retribution is distinguished from revenge. ○ Retribution is a moral demand, not to be confused with utilitarian justifications of punishment. The retributive impulse *limits* punishment as much as it calls for it. ○ Retribution competes with love as a prescribed response to wrong-doing. The retributive impulse appears stronger. ○ It is hypothesized that the retributive impulse is strengthened by a sense of "moral distance." ○ Arguments for determinism and for therapy as substitutes for retribution are advanced and criticized. • Restitution asks for compensation from the predator to his/her victim. ○ Restitution is distinguished from impersonal victim-compensation. ○ Restitutive programs suffer from five difficulties. These difficulties limit the role restitution can play in response to crime.

CRIME PROVOKES RESPONSE. This is particularly true of those crimes that hurt us directly and immediately. But it is also true of those wrongs that wound us at a distance—that offend our morals and that seem to damage the social fabric.

Citizens wish to see "something done" about crime, but in modern states the doing is the job of government. Crime, by definitiion, consists of those wrongs "pursued" by the state, rather than by the injured individual and his or her friends.

The state consists of persons, of course, and the laws it administers have also been produced by individuals. Individuals who make laws, and citizens who support them, justify their legislation. They give *reasons* which, we have seen (Chapter 2, Volume One), are not to be confused with *causes* of their acts.

Reasons given to justify public policies usually employ to two tangled standards: That of rightness and that of correctness. Social policies are to be both humane and efficient. They are to be both moral and rational.

Conflict

These two standards are often fused. Morals set some of the *ends* of action, but they also limit the *means* to be used in achieving those ends.

To "know what we are doing" in response to crime requires ability to separate moral from practical justifications. It requires being able to tell the difference between a moral prescription and an empirical proposition. It requires recognition that one can be moral without being practical and, conversely, that one can be practical without being moral (p. 9). To "know what one is doing" is to be able to tell whether a preferred course of action is desired regardless . . . , or whether it is desired as an efficient means toward some end.

This recommended separation is artificial. While it is required for "knowing what we are doing," it does not occur spontaneously in everyday situations.[1] In everyday action, people characteristically justify their morals with reference to consequences, but, if pressed, moral persons reach a point at which justificatory regress stops and

---

[1] Collingwood (1977, pp. 49–50) assures us that "The first rule of philosophical method . . . [is] to beware of false disjunctions and to assume that the specific classes of a philosophical concept are always liable to overlap, so that two or more specifically differing concepts may be exemplified in the same instances."

In the present context, Collingwood's statement means that the concept, "morality," overlaps the concept, "rationality." Some of the ends of action are morally saturated. Some of the judgments of efficacy of means (rationality) are also morally affected. Nevertheless, *knowing* what one is doing requires ability to separate preference from consequence, value from fact.

they then object to a course of action simply "because it is wrong." And "wrong" here means "even if the proposed action succeeds."

To repeat, then, recognition of the difference between preference and proposition is useful as a means of illuminating conflicts between *what we say* we want to achieve, *what we are willing to do,* and *what we do.*

For example, surveys of public opinion repeatedly reveal that citizens say they want offenders punished *and* reformed. They want criminals imprisoned "to protect society" at the same time that they recognize that "prisons do not help criminals become better people" (R.J. Moore 1980, p. 25).

Conflict between professed ends and selected means is hardly novel. It is apparent *within* individuals, but it is even more apparent *between* individuals. Democratic policies that would be both moral and practical are difficult to develop.

The Paradox of Social Choice

The difficulty of democratic procedure lies in the fact that there is no uncompromising way by which individuals with discrete hierarchies of preferences can combine their "votes" to produce a rational social choice. This phenomenon is known as *Arrow's Impossibility Theorem* after its inventor and demonstrator, the economist Kenneth J. Arrow (1974, 1978; also see MacKay 1980).

Arrow proves that, given some reasonable assumptions about the meaning of rationality, there can be no purely rational device with which to aggregate varied rankings of individual preferences into social choice. While *individuals* can approximate logical consistency in their preferences, no instrument is available with which to vote a host of differing preference hierarchies into a rational *collective* decision.

On a simple level, the "paradox of voting" can be illustrated by a group of three persons who have three options for action. Arrow comments (1978, p. 3):

> Suppose that individual 1 prefers A to B and B to C (and therefore A to C), individual 2 prefers B to C and C to A (and therefore B to A), and individual 3 prefers C to A and A to B (and therefore C to B). Then a majority prefer A to B, and a majority prefer B to C. We may therefore say that the community prefers A to B and B to C. If the community is to be regarded as behaving rationally, we are forced to say that A is preferred to C. But in fact a majority of the community prefer C to A. So the

method just outlined for passing from individual to collective tastes fails to satisfy the condition of rationality, as we ordinarily understand it.

Arrow's statement may be depicted as in Figure 1.1.

Figure 1.1 Schema of "The Paradox of Social Choice"

Person

1 Prefers A > B > C   Therefore, #1 should prefer A > C
2 Prefers B > C > A   Therefore, #2 should prefer B > A
3 Prefers C > A > B   Therefore, #3 should prefer C > B

Majority prefers A > B and B > C
Therefore, this group, if rational, should prefer A > C
But, in fact, majority prefers C > A

Failure to satisfy conditions of rationality is common in the deliberations of committees and Congresses. It applies to domestic quarrels and decisions, and, as MacKay (1980) shows, such failure is also a possibility in the scoring of athletic events. Irrational group decision-making is potential whenever individuals with different orders of preferences try to vote their tastes toward a rational social policy.

The paradox deepens, however, if we complicate the illustration by weighting the individual choices by their *intensity*. Attempting to aggregate individual rankings of choice weighted by their varying intensities makes rational social choice even more problematic. One runs into the issue of how to "score" the desires of "the apathetic majority" against the desires of "the desperate minority," to use MacKay's language (1980, p. 48). The problem then becomes the irresolvable one of how rationally to compare the values of different individuals' wishes. For this reason, Arrow's theorem ignores intensity and addresses only the impossibility of moving from varied individual hierarchies of preferences to a collective social choice that satisfies canons of rationality. Arrow concludes (1974, p. 25):

> Attempts to form social judgments by aggregating individual expressed preferences always lead to the possibility of paradox. Thus there cannot be a completely consistent meaning to collective rationality. We have at some point a relation of pure power.

Other scholars have added to Arrow's indications of the limits of rationality by showing that decisions vary with the way in which possibilities are framed. For example, Tversky and Kahneman's (1981) fascinating experiments demonstrate how it is possible to induce irrational choices and reversals of preferences by phrasing the same "decision problem" in different contexts. Their findings apply to a gamut of decisions—from making purchases to betting on games and on lives.

Relevance

The paradox of social choice is relevant to discussions of response to crime because, in democracies, people do not want just one thing and they do not vote for the same ordering of governmental actions. Although we have no measure of the intensities with which individuals rank options in responding to crime, there is sufficient disagreement in their orders of preference as to make a purely rational public policy ideal rather than real.

Conflict is apparent from a mere listing of avowed objectives of the criminal law, and it is apparent without discussing *how* these objectives are to be achieved. Ignorance of the efficiency of means is yet another obstacle to rational social policy. Furthermore, as the next chapter will argue, conceptions of fair response to crime vary with how the crime is depicted, as per Tversky and Kahneman's experiments.

WHY RESPOND TO CRIME?

The impossibility theorem applies, with special force, to the development of social policy in response to crime. All policies compromise someone's preferred ranking of *objectives* and they also compromise the *means* to be used in achieving those objectives.

Compromise is not just a function of different people wanting different things. It is also a function of crime producing within each citizen and between citizens a *mixture* of practical demand constrained by moral sentiment.

If we ask the radical question, "Why do anything about crime?", the usual reply is that we respond to crime in order to do justice and to protect society. These objectives are not simple and the means invoked under each justification sometimes overlap.

For example, demand for justice asks for several things: That criminal law be fairly produced and applied, and that there be arrest, reprobation, retribution, and, if possible, restitution.

Demand for social protection also calls for several things. It is partly satisfied by arrest and by reprobation. Reprobation presumably also provides social defense by producing a moral revivification through legal symbolism and formal condemnation of the criminal. This moral refreshment—a reminder of what we favor and oppose—is deemed to be socially protective. Formal condemnation is assumed to have an educational effect and to provide a "societal cement," particularly as the criminal law is applied by large majorities against small minorities.

Desire for social protection also aims to reduce crime through incarceration, expulsion, or execution. In addition, efforts are made to reduce crime by correcting the offender. Last, demand for social protection tries to reduce crime by producing deterrent effects, general and specific, and by preventing criminal activity.

Diversity and Collective Rationality

The *hierarchy* of these many demands and the *forms* they take vary between individuals, and they vary more dramatically as culturally heterogeneous people try to live together under one set of laws. Under such circumstances, no system of response to crime can be rationally devised.

By contrast, communities—by which is meant gatherings of individuals of like moral and practical persuasion—may approximate rationality in responding to crime. It is easier for Hutterites or Saudi Arabians to respond consistently to crime than it is for Americans or Canadians. Diversity reduces collective rationality.

Nevertheless, as students, we like to know what we, and our laws, are doing in the hope that this information may move us toward more humane and efficient responses to crime. Therefore, the meanings of popular justifications in reaction to crime deserve comment. Justifications in satisfaction of a sense of justice are the topics of this and the following chapter. Chapters 3, 4, and 5 discuss justifications that refer to societal protection.

DEMAND FOR JUSTICE

Justice is a moral ideal and one with many facets. Cries for justice are not appeals for one quality of act or condition (Nettler 1979). In response to crime, satisfaction of justice asks for several activities, of varied salience, for different individuals.

Arrest

Justice calls for arrest. To arrest means *to stop*. For some time at least, we wish to incapacitate the bad actor.

To arrest also means to *say* "stop" to the present offender and to possible future ones. Arrest is a "holding action" and an important one. Its function as a warning becomes, then, one means of deterring the apprehended person and other potential offenders.

Arrest As Deterrent

Some unknown proportion of possible offenders is assumed to be deterred from cheating and stealing by their conceptions of the shameful consequences of being apprehended—quite apart from any additional punishment. For example, Rettig and Pasamanick (1964) gave American students an impossible task to perform and unobtrusively recorded whether or not they cheated when motivated by money and the suggestions of a confederate. The investigators tested the relative contributions of six factors that might influence cheating: Expectation of gain, the value attached to that expected gain, expectation of censure (being caught and shamed), the value attached to expectation of censure, the judged severity of the offense, and the "reference group" that would suffer from the offense. All of these factors, except the reference group, had an effect, but the value the actor assigned to possibly being shamed accounted for as much of the variation in behavior as the other four factors combined.

In parallel with this finding, Willcock (1974) asked 808 English youths, 15 to 21 years of age, "Which of these things would worry you most about being found out by the police?" Most young men listed as their first worry, "What would the family think about it." Second and third ranks were given to, "The chances of losing my job," and "The publicity or shame of having to appear in court." The punishment that might follow arrest was ranked fourth among these youths' concerns, and this ranking was much the same whether the respondents had admitted to many offenses or few. Given the hypothetical choice between paying a large fine if guilty *without* appearing in court and paying half the fine if one appeared in court, half of Willcock's youths said they preferred to pay the larger fine rather than go to court. Willcock concludes that, "To a marked extent court appearance *in itself* seems to be an important part of the penalty." (p. xxi, emphasis his).

Arrest shames and shame deters, but what is left unanswered by studies such as these is who is deterred how much from which offense by fear of apprehension. As with much theorizing and research about deterrence (Chapter 5), we assume an inhibitory effect of the shame of apprehension without being able to weigh it.

Arrest As Therapy

Arrest is also therapeutic for some kinds of offenders. If the test of a correctional process is cessation of criminal activity, then arrest is itself reformative of some neurotic thieves, most embezzlers, and most unhappy spouse-killers. Arrest ruptures connections—with people and situations—and it provides "the sharp rap" and "the fresh start" that put such careers on a different course.

Arrest As Justice

These possible practical effects of arrest should not be confused with the moral demand for arrest. A common sense of justice asks that the predator be stopped, regardless of auxiliary consequences of that arrest. Arrest is an end in itself, whether or not it is also a means to other ends.

Reprobation

Reprobation is condemnation. A common sense of justice demands that criminal acts be condemned. To reprobate is to indicate by public action that such activity is disapproved. Disapproval is demonstrated by imposing pain upon the "bad" actor.

The pain may vary, of course, from remonstrance and shaming, to flogging, mutilation, incarceration, exclusion, and execution. Restitution also expresses condemnation and imposes the pain of repayment.

There are many pains imposed by government, however, that are *not* deemed to be punitive—a multitude of regulations, for example, and taxes. It is alleged that punishment can be distinguished from penalty by its reprobative function (Feinberg 1970, Chapter 5). Whether this distinction is always discernible or not, punishment is *intended* to express resentment (Berns 1979).

Expression may relieve resentment, but it may also be educative. Punishing what we oppose reinforces our moral sentiment. In some cases, it may also inhibit future bad action and, in this sense, be reformative.

Whether or not these side-effects occur, reprobation is *an end in itself.* Expression of disapproval is a *moral* demand, desired regardless of its consequences. This "ultimacy" is one aspect of moral action, as contrasted with purely practical action. The distinction deserves comment.

Morality and Practicality

The study of morals addresses three sets of questions. One set is *normative:* It asks *what* people should or should not do, and it asks how these mandates can be justified. A second question is *descriptive:* It asks for a statement of the *content* of a moral code, without judging whether that code is, or is not, well justified. A third question calls for *definition:* It asks *what distinguishes* a moral code and moral action from other kinds of statement and action.

Present interest requires attention only to the last issue, an issue that is important because the nature of moral demands ought not to be confused with practical interests *if* we wish to know what we are doing.

John Ladd (1957) has given us one of the clearest definitions of a moral code. He shows that a moral statement is a *prescription for conduct that claims "superiority and legitimacy."*

The *superiority* of a moral code refers to its autonomy, sufficiency, and priority. *Autonomy* means that a moral commandment cannot be justified non-morally. It is an ultimate. *Sufficiency* refers to recognition by members of the group that they are obligated to follow the prescription and that recognition of obligation provides sufficient reason for doing so. *Priority* refers to the fact that a moral code demands *precedence* over other lines of conduct.

The *legitimacy* of a moral code also rests on three attributes. First, a moral code is believed by its advocates to be *possible of justification,* even when no justification is given. Second, the code is held to be *intersubjectively valid.* This means that the code is considered equally binding upon oneself and others. In this sense, a moral code is "impersonal" and "social." To speak of an *individual* moral code is therefore a corruption of the meaning of morality.

The word, "moral," derives from the Latin, *mos* (sing.), *mores* (plural), referring to custom(s). Morals are mandates for groups, and an individual whose ethic contradicts the mores of his/her tribe may be considered immoral according to its canons.

Last, and most frequently confusing, a moral code claims the possibility of justifying itself by reference to *reality.* Ladd points out that moral codes are alleged to be founded on:

> ... the nature of things. This requires that they be in some way derived from man's conception of human nature, or of the world, or of reality in general. ... Every ethical system must have such a foundation, although, of course, moral prescriptions cannot strictly be deduced from it without committing the so-called "naturalistic fallacy" (the fallacy of deducing a prescriptive from a non-prescriptive statement (1957, p. 106).

This definition tells us that morality is *not* dependent upon knowledge, although codes may move, in some uncertain way, with information and they are justified by some appeal to "reality." Furthermore, the superiority and legitimacy of a moral code stimulate resentment against those who break it. Indeed, if persons lack the capacity for indignation and its allied sentiments of remorse and penance, their moral beliefs become vacuous.

In summary, to be moral is to feel resentment at breaches of the code to which one subscribes. Moreover, devotion to the code does not wait upon its practical test. Some code of morals is a requirement of social life, but moral codes are not invented anew as "evaluation research" tests the immediate and distant consequences of a group's moral practices. There may, in fact, be "suicidal ethics," codes that work *against* efficiency and survival.

The philosopher Ludwig Wittgenstein (1922) advised us that, "It is impossible for there to be propositions of ethics." To assume the contrary—to assume that moral codes are validated, or invalidated, by their efficacy in achieving some objective other than that of societal unity—is to confuse moral prescription with empirical proposition. Against this confusion, we are reminded that moral sentiments are *not* reducible to statements of consequences. They do not change in any regular fashion with demonstrable consequences of their subscription. Thus, surveys of American and Canadian public opinion indicate that a majority of those who approve of capital punishment would continue to do so even if the death penalty had no deterrent value (Vidmar 1974, Vidmar & Ellsworth 1974).

Relevance

This point is relevant to the present discussion of the demand for condemnation as part of the demand for justice. It is also relevant to arguments about the utility of different modes of societal protection. For example, the question about capital punishment as a general deterrent usually confounds moral belief and practical result (Chapter 5).

To know what one is doing is to be able to tell the difference between acting efficiently and acting morally. In moral codes there is a terminus beyond which justification is *not* sought. This end-point describes which means cannot be used, regardless of their efficacy.

Retribution

Comments on morality are pertinent to another aspect of the demand for justice. This is the call for retribution. It follows easily from the demand for reprobation and it is probably the most universal claim for justice in response to crime.

The retributive impulse asks that wrongs not go unpunished. Silence in response to crime is itself deemed immoral and therefore unjust.

It is this impulse that is exhibited today in hunts for "war criminals" 40 years after they committed their "crimes." The search serves no deterrent function, but it satisfies the educational function of reminding us of what we oppose and it satisfies the perennial urge to see that wrongs not go unanswered.

Retribution, Not Revenge

Some contemporary moralists have condemned the retributive call for justice by confusing it with revenge. Retribution, however, differs from revenge. Retribution, like restitution, is a sentiment that asks that wrongs be somehow balanced. If an original condition cannot be restored, then the retributive impulse requires that the offender receive a harm for the harm he or she has done.

Three intertwined features mark the difference between retribution and revenge: Disinterest, due process, and balance.

Revenge is "personal." The injured party, or his allies, avenge the wrong. Vendetta may pit one against one or clan against clan. By contrast, retribution is relatively impersonal. Disinterested parties are asked to intervene and redress the wrong. The legal work of retribution therefore operates with due process whereas revenge is not concerned with a third party's judicious weighing of the wrong done.

This means, in turn, that retribution seeks to *balance* the wrong done the victim with the pain consciously administered to the offender. Revenge, however, knows no balance. Vengeance rampages. It incites the retaliation that retribution is designed to quiet. Therefore, in the codes of most civilizations but not all tribes, revenge is deemed to be unjust and retribution, just.

An "Eye-for-an-Eye"

Hammurabi (1792–1750 B.C.), the Babylonian king, gave classic expression to the moral balancing demanded by a retributive sense of justice with his "law of talion" (*lex talionis*), the principle of returning "like-for-like." The Old Testament of the Bible also expresses this sentiment. According to the book of Leviticus (24:17–20), Moses commanded that:

> . . . he that killeth any man shall surely be put to death. And he that killeth a beast shall make it good; beast for beast. And if a man cause a blemish in his neighbor; as he hath done, so shall it be done to him *again*.

Islamic law also asks for retirbution. In a revised version being considered by the Iranian parliament:

Private citizens will be allowed personal retribution against an offender, rather than let the state punish him.

Under Article 53 . . . dealing exclusively with murder and other acts of violence causing injury, the next-of-kin of a murder victim can choose to carry out the execution himself. In the case of injury, the bill says the victim can inflict equal damage as punishment.

"In response to dismemberment of a right hand, the right hand of the offender should be cut off," the bill says.

"If the offender has no right hand, his left hand may be cut off. If he has no hands, his foot may be cut off."

The victim can waive his right to punish the assailant, and waive the right to have the assailant punished at all (Canadian Press 1981).

Retribution As Moral Demand

It is important to note that the retributive sense of justice is *not* evaluated, or diminished, by its consequences. It is a *moral* demand. It is an end in itself, and it matters not which crimes offend which persons because all persons, except rare hermits, demand that some wrongs be answered with pains.

Even individuals who tell us that they reject the retributive impulse exhibit it when they are confronted with heinous crimes. This has been demonstrated in the artificial setting of the college classroom, in public opinion research, and in observation of actual jury work (Kalven & Zeisel 1966, Sharp & Otto 1910, Sherwood 1966, Vidmar 1974, Vidmar & Crinklaw 1973, Vidmar & Miller 1980).

More than this, Posner (1980) believes that there is a *biological basis* for the demand for retribution and that people obtain "economic utility from inflicting injury on people who have injured them" (p. 92, fn. 65).

Whether or not Posner is correct, we note that many criminologists in the Western world who are reluctant to justify responding to crime on retributive grounds, or even on deterrent grounds, nevertheless feel that some serious crimes *deserve* reprobation and retribution.

Thus the distinguished British jurist Barbara Wootton (1978, pp. 246–247) "shudders at the thought [that] the purpose of imprisonment for crime is punishment," as a recent California statute states. She holds, on the contrary, that "the only unchallengeable justification for locking anybody up [is the] likelihood that a prisoner would be a danger . . . to other people if he was released." But, in the same paragraph, Lady Wootton claims that "for such crimes [as aggravated assault and murder] the courts must impose long sentences, even if experience has shown that certain murderers may not actually be serious risks."

In a similar vein, the criminologist Norval Morris (1977) argues that:

> We . . . ought to send to prison those people who deserve to go there by the nature of their crimes. If any lesser punishment would depreciate the seriousness of the crime, then imprisonment is appropriate. The easiest way to state this is by example. Take the usual spouse-killer. He has solved his problem . . . by eliminating his spouse. He is not likely to murder again. Given that truth, we do not need to lock him up to save lives. Suppose, for the sake of argument, that we could show that probation is appropriate here, since imprisonment would not reduce the incidence of spouse-killing. We would still send the spouse-killer to prison. We would impose our maximum punishment as a means of affirming minimum standards of behavior independently of any other social consequences. Every system in the world would impose its maximum punishment in some form or other at this point. . . . In the context of punishment and social control, the concept of just deserts is a proper one. We send people to prison because, given the nature of their crimes, they deserve it (pp. 157–158).

The quality of demand for retribution is well expressed by the philosopher Hannah Arendt (1964) in her study of the Israeli trial and hanging of the Nazi bureaucrat Eichmann. Arendt justifies this expensive ritual by saying, "To the question most commonly asked about the Eichmann trial: 'What good does it do?,' there is but one possible answer: It will do justice" (p. 254).

The criminal law is not merely practical; it is also symbolic. *It expresses morals as well as it intends results.*

Justice, Not Utility

Retribution is a *moral motive* for punishing offenders. It is autonomous. It is not to be confused with the utilitarian justification of punishment as an instrument with which to maximize a vaguely conceived "social welfare."

For example, Carr-Hill and Stern (1979) show that a retributive (balancing) sense of justice accounts for the fact that punishments "seek a certain level" and are *not* increased as a strictly utilitarian, cost-benefit analysis would predict. The retributive impulse *limits* punishment as much as it calls for punishment.

Cost-efficient considerations have some influence, but probably a minor influence, in determining the level of punishment and its style. Conceptions of justice intrude, and Carr-Hill and Stern are able to demonstrate that retribution "does play an important role in actual sentencing systems (and, as far as we can see, in plausible alternatives) " (pp. 291–292).

In summary, response to crime is not produced by an economic calculation of how much crime is deterred by how much punishment of which sort. Response to crime is strongly motivated by a people's sense of justice which, like all else, is subject to change.

Love, Retribution, and Justice

There are philosophers, of course, who ask that wrongs be answered otherwise than with retribution or economic calculation of deterrent effects. They recommend responding to crimes, and other wrongs, with love. However, critics observe two things about this prescription: (a) that the majority of its nominal advocates do not apply it, and (b) that most human beings do not accept it.

Retribution and love have a long history of conflict as just responses to wrongs (Kelsen 1957, pp. 35–40). Indeed, some philosophers and psychologists have noted that "love and justice are antagonistic virtues" (Pateman 1980, p. 24). Love, it is claimed, is particularistic and therefore in conflict with the requirements of justice which demand, in Pateman's words, that "private interests be subordinated to the public . . . good."

Morality and Justice

Scholars such as Wootton, Morris, and Arendt clearly voice the moral, and non-utilitarian, sense of justice that calls for retribution. It does *not* diminish the morality of this demand that any of its appeals to facts—justifications by appeals to reality—may be incorrect. For example, Morris's statement that "every system in the world imposes its maximum punishment" for domestic homicide is, as we have seen (Volume Two), incorrect. To the contrary, we are reminded that grand juries in Harris County, Texas, dismiss charges in about *half* of all homicide incidents brought before them (Lundsgaarde 1977), and that most of these dismissed cases involve killings between acquaintances or intimates. In addition, we note that Islamic law, as applied in Iran, declares some murderers justified and not to be punished, as when one man kills another for insulting a prophet or saint, or when a husband kills his wife and her lover whom he has caught copulating (Canadian Press 1981).

Hypothesis

The retributive impulse seems, then, to be universal, but the quality of crime that stimulates it varies with moralities. However, there

CHAPTER **1** DOING JUSTICE   15

may be a universal feature of the retributive urge that can be phrased as a hypothesis yet to be tested. It is the possibility that the retributive impulse is stronger, the greater the "moral distance" between observer and offender.

"Moral distance" refers to the subjective sense that the offender's crime is, or is not, our possibility. The hypothesis is that crimes that seem to be outside the range of our possibility excite the most resentment. Conversely, crimes committed by "people like us"—that are felt to be "the kind of thing" we could do—stimulate less resentment and less demand for retribution.[2]

This hypothesis does not claim "moral distance" to be the only factor affecting the call for retribution.[3] It holds only that, other contengencies equal, appreciation of this kind of psychic similarity-dissimilarity between observer and offender influences observers' sense of justice and the impulse to condemn and punish.

Criticism and Conclusion

The retributive impulse is itself condemned by some philosophers. For example, Anatol Rapoport (1950, p. 229) believes that "the whole notion of 'justice' " will change as scientific ways of thinking become more popular. With such change, according to Rapoport, " 'revenge' [and presumably retribution] . . . becomes as senseless as beating a piece of furniture one has bumped into. So does the punishment of crime." Rapoport contends that:

> The scientist by his study of the world constantly strives to make it appear more "predetermined" by making it more predictable. The "crimi-

---

[2] The concept of "moral distance" is psychological. It is not to be confused with Black's (1976) thesis about "the behavior of law," according to which "social distance" affects application of law where "social distance" is recognized by markers of social rank.

Empirical test of Black's theory finds it only modestly correct and to have low power to predict legal response to criminal conduct (Myers 1980a). By contrast, Gottfredson and Hindelang's hypothesis (1979a, 1979b, 1980) receives slightly greater empirical support. This hypothesis contends that law responds principally to the degree of harm an offender inflicts upon a victim. For some kinds of crime, such as robbery and rape, the harm factor operates to determine severity of prosecution. However, "harm," measured by amount of property lost, *decreases* the likelihood of a guilty verdict (Myers 1980, p. 849).

Criminal law is applied in a web of circumstances and, as this chapter argues, no one factor need explain all variations in legal response to crime.

[3] My colleague, Robert Silverman, suggests that the moral distance hypothesis applies even more strongly to revenge than to retribution.

nal," therefore, appears to the scientist *not* free, inasmuch as he can be made the object of study. It becomes meaningless, therefore, for the scientist to separate aberrations of "physiological" functions, commonly recognized as disease, from those "psychological" aberrations which are still labeled in our prescientific legal language as "crime." There is no room in the ethical system of the scientist for such concepts as "paying the debt to society," "redemption of sin," "retribution," etc., and for all the morbid aspects of religious ethics that are commonly associated with those concepts. (pp. 229-230, emphasis his).

In similar vein, the psychiatrist Karl Menninger (1968) calls punishment a "crime." His thesis is that we now have knowledge with which to correct most offenders and that it is inhumane, therefore, to punish criminals when we could reform them.

"Do I believe there is effective treatment for offenders," he asks, "and that they *can* be changed? *Most certainly and definitely I do* (p. 261, emphasis his).

"There really *is* such a thing as behavioral science," he adds (p. 17, emphasis his). Therefore, he concludes, "being against punishment is not a sentimental conviction. It is a logical conclusion drawn from scientific experience" (p. 204).

Doubts

Unfortunately for these arguments, no society can function on the assumption of complete determinism of human action nor is there so much science in the study of human behavior as is claimed.

Determinism is not an assumption that can be invoked for bad actors, but not for good ones. Once assumed, determinism applies to everyone, not just to "criminals." Rapoport's beliefs become as much "predetermined" as a robber's acts. By Rapoport's reasoning, if all acts are caused, then neither praise nor blame can be justified.

But praise and blame *do* things. They have consequences as reinforcers of preferred styles of life. They are among the determinants—or demi-determinants—of our actions. For the foreseeable future, these reinforcements will continue to be employed, and they will be employed "naturally," which means less than efficiently.

Menninger's claims are also defective. The study of human behavior is not as scientific as he contends. Chapters 1–7 in Volume One describe some of the limitations. Furthermore, as Chapter 6 will make clear, it remains a matter of conjecture *how much* correctional power resides with practitioners of psychiatry, psychology, and related disciplines.

Here it can be noted that Menninger's preferred psychoanalytic techniques have *no demonstrable value,* other than that of providing comfort for some subscribers (Rachman & Wilson 1980, Chapter 5). A million-dollar, in-house study, the Menninger Clinic Report, traced psychotherapeutic outcomes over 14 years (Appelbaum 1977). The findings do *not* justify Menninger's claims of curative powers.

We expect that retribution will continue to be demanded as a requirement of justice, although the mode in which it is expressed may vary. Saying this recommends nothing; the statement is only descriptive.

Restitution

In addition to demands for arrest, reprobation, and retribution, a persistent sense of justice asks that those who do us wrong restore us to our condition before that wrong. Restitution demands compensation. It calls for return to our status before the crime and it requires that the criminal, rather than some surrogate, complete the restoration. The call for restitution is easier to satisfy, of course, for damage to property than for damage to person.

Restitution: More Than Victim-Compensation

Involvement of offenders in restoration of their victims marks a difference between restitution as a response to crime and simple victim-compensation. Governments are increasingly establishing agencies to compensate victims of crime out of tax revenues. While this assistance to victims is laudable if affordable, it lacks a component of the notion of restitution—namely, the idea that offenders "make it up" to their victims.

A reason for emphasizing offender's repayment is that such restitution becomes part of the "treatment" of the criminal and substitutes for other forms of punishment. On moral grounds, as well as economic grounds, restitution, when it can be effected, makes the offender responsible for his or her conduct. Thus, Kathleen Smith (1965), a former assistant governor of Holloway Prison in England, urges that all able-bodied inmates determine the length of their sentences by the amount of their earnings contributed in restoration of their victims—whether the earnings be from prison jobs or from extramural work. Smith supports her case with economic and humane arguments, but also by the presumed rehabilitative effects or restitutive acts upon offenders.

Smith's "cure for crime," as she calls it, would satisfy one important element in the demand for justice, but few states have acted upon her prescription because of the difficulties of implementation. The criminal codes of many Western countries allow for restitution as part of a sentence, but offenders' compensation of victims plays only a small part in sentencing practice. For example, The Canadian Criminal Code allows for restitution to be made in sentencing:

1. as part of a probation order;
2. to restore damage to property in amounts less than $50;
3. when a person convicted of an indictable offense has sold stolen property to an innocent third party. Upon restoration of the property to its rightful owner, the offender may be ordered to repay the purchaser of his/her stolen goods;
4. when an accused is tried for an indictable offense (felony) and *not* convicted of it, but:

> the court finds that in indictable offence has been committed, the court may order that any property obtained by the commission of the offence shall be restored to the person entitled to it, if at the time of the trial the property is before the court or has been detained, so that it can be immediately restored to that person under the order (Sec. 655–2).

5. when the victim of a felony applies to the court for restitution at the time of sentencing of his/her predator.

Other jurisdictions make similar, if not identical, allowances for restitution. However, surveys of sentencing practices reveal that restitutive contracts are infrequently used in formal procedures (Law Reform Commission of Canada 1974). Nevertheless, it is believed that "restitution is often made informally prior to sentencing in the hope that it will result in a more lenient sentence" (Griffiths et al. 1980, p. 186).

No tallies are available of pre-sentence offers to make restitution in mitigation of sentence or of the consequences of such offers. Such observation would make interesting research. Meanwhile, Klein's (1976) interviews with 115 Canadian convicts about their experiences with "plea-bargaining" demonstrate the uncertainties of restitution as a sentence option. Klein reports cases in which promises of lenient sentence upon restoration of stolen property were broken and he indicates that, for some offenders, the trade-off between estimated time to be served and property to be retained favors keeping stolen wealth. He writes:

> "Ted" is regarded by systematic cheque forgers as one of the best in the business. In a period of less than two months, he cashed over $100,000

worth of forged certified cheques. As has been the case with many systematic cheque forgers, his arrest came about as a result of chance rather than through scientific detective work: He was stopped for a traffic violation. . . . At the time of his arrest, the police promised him a lenient sentence if he would return the proceeds of his cheque-writing spree. "Ted" simply could not see the percentage in such a deal. He felt certain that, given the publicity associated with the case, he would get at least a five-year sentence even if he returned the money. Without returning the money, he estimated that the most time he would get would be ten years, given the sentencing patterns in the jurisdiction where he was arrested. In "Ted's" estimation, one-hundred thousand, well-laundered, tax-free dollars were worth more than what, at most, would be a five-year difference in the amount of time to be served. He refused to return the money and was given a seven-year sentence (p. 22).

Troubles With Restitution

While the objectives of a restitutive sentence are admirable, dispute continues about the justice and efficacy of procedures for implementing such sentences.

During the 1970s the Law Enforcement Assistance Administration in the United States and the Solicitor Generals of Canada and Alberta sponsored experimental projects of restitution, but there has been no general assessment of their utility. As a consequence, differing evaluations are presented from different jurisdictions. Thus Burt Galaway (1977) and his colleagues in Minnesota (Hudson et al. 1977) report favorably on their experiences although they present no tallies of consequences. On the other hand, John Klein (1980), director of the Pilot Alberta Research Centre (PARC) from 1975 to 1977, believes that restitutive sentencing cannot be the sole mode, or even the principal mode, of response to crime.

The justice of the restitutive principle is admitted, but difficulties in implementation deserve recognition. These difficulties include the following troubles: 1. who shall determine amounts to be paid?; 2. how shall psychic pain and physical injury be valued?; 3. does restitution rehabilitate offenders?; 4. is restitution a bribe paid for lenience?; and 5. are restitutive contracts feasible?

1. Who shall determine the amount to be restored and how shall the determination be calculated?

Two procedures have been tried—arbitration and negotiation. The arbiter is presumed to be a neutral observer, usually a judge or probation officer, who is informed of the nature of the loss by both offender and victim and whose judgment is binding on both. The victim may, of course, still sue for damages in civil court. Negotiation brings offender and victim together with a neutral third party in an attempt to construct a restitutive contract.

Arbitration is quicker and neater than negotiation. However, Galaway (1980, p. 273) assumes that negotiation will produce agreements conceived by both parties to be just and that communication between criminal and his/her victim "should reduce stereotypes which they may have held of each other." Galaway provides no evidence of these benign effects and there is as much reason to believe that communication will confirm a stereotype as that it will disconfirm it. But, on this point, Klein's (1980, p. 296) findings from the restitutive project in Alberta show that "very few victims would even give serious consideration to having the offender work for them, let alone having any contact with the offender."

Troubles in determining compensation are compounded by "hard cases" in which more than one offender is involved or in which victim's judgment of loss is (typically) higher than offender's judgment of "take." A criminal court's ability to make fair assessment can be doubted and a sentence of restitution can be appealed. Appeals add, of course, to the costs of doing justice.

2. How shall psychic pain and physical injury be valued?

Determining just reparation is further confounded by difficulties in assessing the psychic pains of victims and the dollar values of injuries incurred by physical attacks.

Most restitutive orders are made for property offenses but, even with damage to property, the victim suffers some psychological trauma. For example, Bard and Sangrey (1979) have written a *Crime Victim's Book* detailing the shock and the changes in attitudes toward others that result from invasions of one's property as well as from injuries to one's body. For these psychic insults, courts have no remedy.

3. Does restitution rehabilitate offenders?

It is presumed that restitution will not only do justice, but that it will also rehabilitate offenders. There is no evidence of such consequence, and debate proceeds with hypothetical arguments about the likely effects of criminals compensating their victims.

The hypothesis favoring restitution holds that repaying one's victim induces a sense of responsibility which, in turn, lessens propensity to crime. A contrary hypothesis, built upon some socio-psychological research, holds that repaying victims may allow offenders to *justify* themselves and thus to *lessen* their sense of wrong-doing.

This issue remains open. However, Miller (1981) points to a set of disadvantages in requiring restitutive contracts of thieves. Miller selected a group of 419 adult property offenders who were ordered to repay their victims as a condition of probation. He matched this "restitutive group" on 28 variables with a sample of 179 offenders who were not ordered to make restitution. Miller summarizes his findings as follows:

> Compared to those not ordered to repay their victims, the offenders ordered to pay restitution had a more difficult probation experience, having more revocations filed against them and showing a greater frequency of reporting, physical health, and money problems. No difference in arrest rate or time on probation was discovered. Those offenders ordered to pay restitution but who did not pay in full had the greatest problems of all, showing the highest revocation filing and actual revocation rate, rate of convictions, and time served. . . . It was suggested that closer probation officer scrutiny of offenders ordered to pay restitution may have accounted for the more difficult experience of the restitution group and that cost of administration of restitution programs may not be worth the benefits.

4. Is restitution a bribe paid for lenience?

Where a restitutive sentence reduces other punishment, the practice may be considered unjust. Klein (1980, pp. 290–291) calls this "trading dollars for leniency" and claims that the trade, if effected, wrongs the poorer offender. Nevertheless, in the Alberta project, two-thirds of the offenders who entered into a restitutive contract believed that it would result in more lenient treatment by the court.

5. Are restitutive contracts feasible?

A survey of criminal victimization among Americans (Harland 1981) finds that, for some kinds of crime, neither the low wages of offenders nor the amount of damage suffered is an obstacle to a restitutive response. However, this study was concerned only with six "focal offenses":

1. larceny away from home in which property is not taken directly from the victim.
2. larceny from or near the home in which property is not taken directly from the victim.
3. pocket-picking and purse-snatching ("larceny without contact").

    4. vehicle theft.

    5. burglary.

    6. unarmed robbery that includes *only* threats or minor assaults
(Harland 1981, p. 4).

This survey reports that relatively few victims receive compensation for such crimes, either by return of property or through insurance, and that restitutive sentences therefore have an intuitive appeal despite their unsystematic application.

Nevertheless, the feasibility of restorative contracts is challenged by present work-loads of courts and probation officers who have to monitor fulfilment of agreements. It is challenged, too, by the fact that, in the Alberta experiment, one-third of the criminals who accepted a repayment contract reneged on their agreements within the short life of the project.

In addition, implementation of a restitutive contract is impossible when large amounts have been stolen. There is dispute about how many cases would be so affected. For example, in the Minnesota experiment, "the vast majority of restitutive contracts [were negotiated for less than] $200 (Galaway 1980, p. 296). However, in the Alberta test, "21% of the cases involved amounts under $100 while 38% of the referrals involved amounts over $500 (Klein 1980, p. 296).

These proportions refer, of course, to culprits who were involved in the restitutive experiments. They do not refer to all thieves. The growth of theft by computer manipulation means that some minority of thieves steal large amounts. One estimate claims that the average "take" in a computer crime is $430,000 (Law Enforcement Assistance Administration 1979). Another estimate of *federal* computer crimes in the United States puts the average loss at about $30,000 (Committee on Government Operations 1977). Whichever estimate is more nearly correct, restitution of such sums is improbable. Given the tendency of smart "computer-jockeys" to conceal their gains and of others to spend their easy wealth, recovery of stolen money and property is doubtful. For example, the student who instructed a computer to send him equipment from the Pacific Telephone and Telegraph Company stole an estimated one million dollars worth of property. In another, larger "scam," computer-manipulation was used to defraud many industrial magnates and movie luminaries of an estimated $130 million of which only $30 million was recovered (Swanson & Territo 1980, p. 307).

    In such cases, full restitution is impossible and token restitution, less than just.

Summary

It would be economical, and just, if restitutive contracts could assume a larger role in response to crime. Given the enumerated difficulties, this seems unlikely.

Demand for justice includes demand that the criminal law be fairly produced and administered. This is the topic of the next chapter.

2 FAIRNESS IN CRIMINAL LAW

Abstract • Demand for justice is demand that selected wrongs be pursued by the state as crimes. ○ Changing societies experience conflicts about the nomination of wrongs to be treated as crimes. ○ Conflict is reduced as criminologists attend to "classic crimes." ○ In democracies, laws against the "classic crimes" seem fairly produced. • Demand for justice also asks that criminal laws be fairly administered. ○ Fair administration is made difficult by tensions between the ideals of uniform application, individual consideration, and equal result. ○ Resolution of these tensions is complicated by difficulties in ascertaining whether unique events do, or do not, constitute "the same kind of crime." ○ In legal and moral arenas, interests and their conflicts define "events." ○ Social relations assign different meanings to "the same wrongful act." ○ The emotional atmosphere in which some crimes are produced and pursued also complicates definition of unique events as similar or different. • Research that would test for fair administration of the law must include the social context—the pattern of considerations, allowable and excludable, in application of the law. ○ Inclusion of the social context requires attention to shifts in the sense of justice with time and place. ○ In Western countries, tests of the impact of legal and extralegal factors upon criminal disposition find generally that legal factors determine decisions far more than do extralegal biases. ○ Research is reviewed in differential responses to the crimes committed by various ethnic groups. History suggests the possibility of unfair treatment of selected minorities. Contemporary research that would test this possibility has been less than well done. Results vary with time, place, and category of crime. • Individual variations among lawyers, judges, juries, defendants, and victims sometimes produce differential responses to crimes. ○ Judges who are more "legalistic" tend to sentence by offense gravity, rather than by extralegal considerations. ○ Judges' personal characteristics play a minor role in adjudication. ○ Titles and descriptions of crimes make a difference in legal response. ○ Defendant's poverty may influence the justice s(he) receives. ○ The relative attractiveness of defendant and victim may influence verdicts, but results from artificial juries should not be confused with results from actual juries and judges. ○ Judges tend to sentence more severely those defendants who opt for trial by jury, but this possibility has not been well tested. ○ In deciding guilt or innocence, juries tend to be more lenient than judges. ○ Jury size and voting rules produce differences in verdicts. ○ "Blue ribbon" juries may be more competent than juries that are representative of the population. • Wealth and power sometimes distort justice. ○ Justice is best defended when power meets power. ○ Justice is an ideal. This means that we are guided by it, and approximate it, but never fully achieve it.

JUSTICE IN A DEMOCRACY REQUIRES that the state pursue as "crimes" only those acts, and all those acts, deemed to be wrong *and* deserving of government attention.

The inventory of conceivable wrongs is tremendous, of course, and subject to change as morals move and as competing interests make demands of legislators. Thus one hears simultaneous pleas that some old crimes be removed from statute books and some new ones added.

For example, citizens quarrel about whether induced abortion is a "right" or "murder." They debate whether keeping a bawdy house should or should not be criminal, and they disagree about whether "aiding and abetting" suicide should be the concern of the state.

Arguments persist about whether crimes should be made out of driving without a seat belt, riding a bike without a helmet, spreading "hate literature" and pornography, having "too many" children, and selling "harmful" products. Citizens also disagree whether crimes should be created out of commercial monopoly, industrial and personal pollution, "discrimination,"[1] and monetary inflation.

In this age of law-making, Americans have proposed that the transmission of subliminal messages be forbidden (Shack 1980), that it be

---

[1] "Discrimination" is placed in quotation marks because it is used indiscriminately. The word refers to more than one kind of event. What "discrimination" means in studies of perception, for example, is not what it means in studies of social relations. The concept, as it is employed by journalists and social scientists, often has no clear indicator (Becker 1971, Finkelstein 1966, Hagan 1977b, L. Smith 1978, Sowell 1978).

The idea of social discrimination includes "malicious intent" on the part of a perpetrator. In the political arena, such intent is seldom demonstrated when charges of "discrimination" are laid. In place of wrongful intent, *difference* comes to signify "discrimination," however that difference may have been produced (Hoffman & Reed 1981).

Some sociologists define "discrimination" as inequality in some measured attribute, such as income, schooling, or sentencing, "after the contributions to that inequality made by variables other than discrimination have been evaluated" (Duncan 1967, p. 87). This is *not*, of course, a measure of prejudiced practice. And even as an *explanation* of inequality, an index of difference is as adequate, or inadequate, as the causal candidates included in the model of how things come to be as they are.

In sociology, the idea of "discriminatory treatment" refers to social relations in which one party treats another unfairly, usually in order to maintain a position of greater power and privilege. A test of "unfair treatment" requires that a *principle* of fair treatment be specified. Given such a principle, *systematic* violations of it become more valid signs of "discrimination" as these violations are embedded in a history of expressed contempt by one party for another.

illegal to move "monetary instruments" worth more than $5,000 out-side the country without a permit (HR-5961), that it be a crime to dis-close the identities of U.S. "intelligence agents" (*National Review* 1980b), that executives be held personally liable for crimes of their corporations, whether or not they had planned the act or taken part in it (Schellhardt 1978), that it be a felony to mail information about abortion (Schellhardt 1978), and that it be an offense to have sexual intercourse without advising one's partner "of all the consequences of the act" (Totaro 1978).

It has also been recommended that "political aggression and racial and sexual inequalities" be considered crimes (Bottomley 1979, p. 36) along with "imperialistic war and poverty" (Schwendinger & Schwendinger 1975). And, in the anarcho-communist tradition ex-pressed by Proudhon's famous dictum that "property is theft," it has been proposed that private property be condemned (Pepinsky 1976) and governments abolished (Tifft & Sullivan 1980).

Classic Crimes

This small sample of demands for production of criminal law sug-gests that the nomination of "crime" has no end. Although nine-teenth century "liberals" wanted to reduce state intervention in the lives of citizens, twentieth century "liberals" urge greater state inter-vention. A difficulty with nineteenth century liberalism is that it seems heartless today, particularly as voluntary self-help associations decline. A difficulty with twentieth century liberalism is that it may be impossible to have the state do things *for* us without having it do things *to* us.

The modern state is that agency with a monopoly of power over a people in a territory.[2] States wield this power with varied instru-ments, including propaganda, education, and taxation (Tussman 1977), but the instrument of last resort is coercion where this ranges from enforced deprivation and loss of "privileges" to imposition of physical and psychological pain.

Criminal law is one arm of coercive control. What is at issue in de-

---

[2] Niccolò Machiavelli (1469–1527) is responsible for the modern idea of the state as an agency with a monopoly of power over those within its territory.

The state is not like a voluntary association that one may join or leave. Ex-clusive of the possibility of migration and naturalization, which states them-selves allow or forbid, individuals have limited powers to adopt or quit "membership" in states (Benn 1967).

mocracies is how the citizenry wishes that force to be used and against which people and which acts.

There are no adequate studies addressing this issue. We have no measures of the balance of demands for the manufacture or reduction of criminal law. Surveys have questioned samples of the population about particular questions—abortion and marijuana, for example—but we lack comprehensive investigation of public conceptions of wrongs to be pursued as crimes:

> We know little about citizens' conceptions of criminal justice and their demand for it. We know little about the *quality* of the sense of justice in different regions—i.e., what people want done in response to crime—or of the *intensity* of demand for justice—i.e., how much people are willing to pay for satisfaction of their sense of justice (Nettler 1979a, p. 46, emphasis in the original).

Lacking information about the full roster of wrongs citizens believe should be crimes, attention is advisably limited to the so-called "classic crimes," those crimes considered wrong-in-themselves (crimes *mala in se*) and which have received general condemnation.

There seems to be nearly universal agreement in defining as crimes such perennial wrongs as murder, manslaughter, forcible rape, assault, robbery, burglary, arson, and a variety of larcenies. For example, Newman (1976) and his associates interviewed samples of rural and urban residents in India, Indonesia, Iran, Italy (Sardinia), Yugoslavia, and the United States (New York) and had them rank nine acts as more or less serious and deserving of state action. Newman's nine acts constitute only a narrow range of possible wrongs, but he found that "respondents in all cultures tended to classify the acts into similar groupings [and that] for traditional crimes, a high degree of consensus was found for their disapproval" (p. 285).

Production of the criminal law in condemnation of the classic crimes seems uncontentious although, as we shall see, *condemnation varies with particular descriptions of these broad categories of wrongs and with the social contexts in which they occur.*

Criminologists raise questions, however, about the advisability of inventing new crimes and the justifications for expanding or contracting definitions of the traditional crimes. For example, proponents of the "conflict" ("radical deviancy" or Marxist) school contend (a) that the definition of crime is imposed upon "the people" by elites and (b) that criminal law in capitalist countries serves "the ruling class" as an instrument of social control.

Those who have advanced these suggestions have done little to test them. But such limited tests indicate, contrary to the radical view, that citizens of democracies share conceptions of acts that deserve to be called crimes and that the production of criminal law is not a monopoly of a "ruling class."

For example, Berk, Brackman, and Lesser (1977) provide a fair test of the latter hypothesis. They studied changes in the California penal code from 1955 to 1971. Their observations of how criminal law is made:

> ... [conforms with] the pluralistic model [of organized interests] emphasized by American political science. ... The content of the California Penal Code responds to a variety of forces having complex synergistic and inhibiting effects. ... [In the legislative arena] no single force dominated and no narrow political persuasion achieved hegemony" (p. 299).

Within the boundaries of crimes *mala in se,* criminal law in republican states seems fairly produced, as judged by citizens. Less agreement is found when we study administration of the law.

FAIR ADMINISTRATION OF THE CRIMINAL LAW

Fair administration of the criminal law is made difficult in democracies by ideals that seek to balance uniform application, individual consideration, and equal result.

Uniform application is the ideal of principled action—the ideal that factors outside the purpose of the law not affect its administration. This objective does *not* call for equal result of the law since each case is deemed to be unique and allowance is to be made for individuality in the persons and circumstances of a crime. To be "equal *before* the law," as the popular maxim puts it, is not to be "equal *after* the law."

The desideratum of uniform application asks only that discretion in application of the law be used according to legal principles, rather than whimsically or prejudicially. Bias in administration of the law is recognized when *extralegal* considerations *systematically* bend responses to offenders.

Difficulties

Tensions between the objectives of *equal* treatment and *individual* treatment, between equal result and discretionary consideration of mitigating circumstances, make it difficult to judge fairness in administration of the criminal law. The difficulty includes that of ascertaining how to define events as "one kind of crime," and this difficulty is compounded by the emotional context in which serious crimes occur.

Flaccid Taxa

Philosophers and jurists try to establish criteria by which to ascertain whether happenings are, or are not, one kind of event. But *it is evolved practice,* rather than philosophic distinction, *that defines events.*

For example, Ian Ross (1981) studied how officials assign "causes of death." He discovered that "physical changes provide evidence that an event has taken place. However, it is not *prima facie* obvious that perceptually identifiable features of physical change *define* something that has happened *as an event"* (p. 37, emphasis added).

In keeping with Ross's statement, social psychologists demonstrate that *how many events* are counted in a sequence of behaviors varies with the subjective *importance* attached to the observation (Russell (1979).

We note the "multi-propertied character of one and the same event . . . the fact that the same action may fall under many different descriptions" (Strawson 1981, p. 127). Thus lawyers and judges struggle with the shifting boundaries of definitions. For example, a tax court recently had to decide whether discounts to favored buyers were "illegal bribes," "kickbacks," or "business costs" (*The Wall Street Journal* 1980e). In another case, the United States Supreme Court split three ways in deciding whether drug enforcement officers had "seized" a narcotics courier, contrary to the Fourth Amendment's prohibition of "unreasonable searches and seizures," or whether they had merely "found" the guilty suspect by "requesting" to search her (Seligman 1980a).

Philosophers are of little help when they advise us that one event is identical with another if both have the same causes and effects (Davidson 1981). *In the legal and moral arenas, interests and their conflicts define "events."*

Social Contexts Define Events

In summary, circumstances and our moral appreciation of them affect definitions of acts as crimes of varied gravity. Moral appreciation varies with the social relations of the actors. All societies of which we have record regard "the same injury" as differing in gravity when it occurs between intimates rather than between strangers. For example, the anthropologists Laura Nader and Harry Todd (1978) bring

together ethnographic reports on the handling of disputes in ten societies around the world. The repeated lesson of these studies is that
quarrels among people who "know" one another and who have an
interest in preserving a valued relationship are settled differently, and
hence construed differently, from contests with "outsiders." In short,
"the same wrong" is more wrong when perpetrated by a stranger
than by one of "our own kind."

Justification

There is practical justification for this distinction. It is that the
wounds strangers inflict upon us hurt more than do the same injuries
intimates produce.

The degree to which this is so, and the conditions under which it
is so, need more research than we have. However, in illustration of
the present point, Ellis and her colleagues (1981) interviewed and
tested 27 adult women who had been raped. These investigators
found that the raped women, when compared with a control group,
suffered, for more than one year after the attack, from what has been
termed "the rape trauma syndrome" (Burgess & Holmstrom 1974).
This syndrome includes depression, anxiety about sex, fear of violence, avoidance of dating, difficulties in interpersonal relations, and,
in general, being less happy day by day. Moreover, in confirmation of
our present thesis, this damaging effect is most pronounced among
those women who had been attacked suddenly and violently *by
strangers*.

Reprise

The fact that "the same crime" appears "more wrong" when committed by a stranger than by an intimate restates a theme expressed in
Volume One, Chapters 4 and 8: That legal categories of crime do *not*
describe homogeneous clusters of acts and actors. Rape and homicide are not one kind of event. Even in its legal sub-categories, such
as "first degree murder" or "negligent manslaughter," "homicide" includes more than one kind of happening.

In illustration of this point, Danet and her colleagues (1980)
analyzed 12 cases heard in various circuits of the United States Courts
of Appeals dealing with putatively the same offense: That of threatening the life of the President—a federal offense. Despite efforts of
legislators to write clear laws specifying well-defined acts as crimes,
the act of "threatening" is vague. In administration of this law, judges
and juries are asked to decide whether a "speech act" constitutes a
"threat" which is illegal or something else.

Citizens and their courts recognize that *saying* is not the same as *intending* and that the meanings of words spoken and words heard vary. What a speaker intends and what an auditor hears are not always identical, and whether a saying is interpreted as a threat depends on circumstances that have to be evaluated judiciously.

Discretion is required, and it is allowed (Wexler 1975). But discretion produces unequal results from attempted uniform application of the law. Some of the inequality will be judged "fair," and some not.

It follows that "bias" in application of the law cannot be rigorously ascertained without a reliable taxonomy of events that categorizes crimes. Such a taxonomy is lacking, and this means that tests of fair play have thus far been crude.

Emotional Atmosphere

Difficulty of definition is compounded by the emotional atmosphere in which publicly visible crimes occur. For example, the sometimes mortal contests engaged by police and culprits make dispassionate justice problematic. Thus, "police brutality" is easy to charge if one ignores provocation. It is no apology for police use of "excessive force" to note that, in the United States and, probably, in other democracies, there is a strong relationship between police violence and public violence. Without specifying which is cause and which effect, Harding and Fahey (1973) observe that killing *by* the police is associated with killing *of* the police.

Use of deadly police power varies with the "toughness" of the areas in which they work (Kania & Mackey 1977), and there is a high correlation between police use of the "strong arm" among different segments of the population and differential rates of violent crime committed by those segments.

These relationships are found for the United States as a whole (Goldkamp 1976) and for particular cities such as Chicago (Harding & Fahey 1973), Birmingham, Detroit, Indianapolis, Kansas City, Oakland, Portland, Oregon, and Washington, D.C. (Milton et al. 1977).

Despite these considerations, the citizenry is sensitive to possible biases in the discretionary activities of agents of the law—police, prosecutors, judges, and juries. Sensitivity is justified by the venerable warning that power is easily abused.

In accord with this sensitivity, criminologists have tested repeatedly for prejudice in administration of the criminal law, with particular reference to possible biases against classes, races, and sexes. Research on this topic is predominantly American, but investigations have also been conducted in Australia, Canada, Great Britain, and New Zealand.

Research Requirement

Evaluations of this research indicate deficiencies in many of these investigations (Hagan 1974a, 1974b, 1975a, 1975b, Nettler 1979a, 1980). A major defect has been lack of attention to the context of decision.

Decisions are produced in social webs. This is true of decisions to arrest, to prosecute, to convict, and to sentence. The social networks in which judgments are made mix considerations of legal and extra-legal factors. Fair tests for prejudice in application of the law need to be alert to this entanglement and powerful enough to disentangle legal from extralegal considerations without damaging the fabric of decision.

Much research has *narrowed* the context of decision by using a few indicators of possible extralegal bias where those indicators are *themselves correlated* with legal considerations. For example, measures of social status and ethnicity are usually considered as irrelevant to discretionary use of the law; they are regarded as extralegal. But, in the disposition of juvenile offenders, these factors are associated with legally relevant considerations such as the quality of parental supervision, the presence of emotional disorder, and commitment to criminality.

To repeat, discretion is employed in a social context that defines justice. Interpretation of the fairness of discretion varies with judgment of the "extenuating circumstances" surrounding each criminal incident. Tests of fair application are adequate, then, only when they look for "the patterned contribution of multiple factors to decisions case-by-case" (Nettler 1979a, p. 41).

What is required of adequate tests for possibly distorted justice is appreciation of the system of judgments within which decisions are made. This means that simultaneous equations methods must be used to represent the system, *not* statistical tests for differences possibly produced by nominated causes weighed one at a time. Equity (fairness) is *not* measured correctly by signs of equality or inequality in judicial result alone.

Example: Two "Prices" for Homicide

This point is illustrated by contrasting interpretations of sentences for homicide in Philadelphia. Zimring, Eigen, and O'Malley (1976) analyzed the distribution of punishment for homicide and concluded that there were two "prices" for this crime in Philadelphia: "wholesale and retail."

> The wholesale price is paid for the majority of killings, those that prosecutors—and presumably the publics behind them—wish to dispose of quickly, usually through plea negotiation, without a jury trial, and with a prison sentence of two years or less. By contrast, the retail price is exacted for homicides that involve concurrent felonies or aggravating circumstances. Aggravating circumstances include such features as the particular vulnerability of the victim or the wanton nature of the crime. Zimring and his associates do not control for the application of these legally relevant factors case-by-case. However, they show that "Black defendants who kill white victims [while committing other felonies] receive the life or death sentence more than twice as often as black felony suspects who kill black victims. These figures must be qualified because black victims are more likely to know black offenders and therefore the crime may not appear to be as wanton as when the offender does not know the victim" (p. 232). Zimring et al. describe the interplay of formal law, its administration, and a public's sense of justice in broad terms only. They sought a "rational theory of punishment" that would produce a unimodal or flat distribution of penalties rather than the bimodal distribution of their Philadelphia data, but "the going price of criminal homicide [in Philadelphia] is either two years or twenty" (p. 251), and they "cannot find the principle that justifies differences of ten-to-one within the general category of murder" (p. 242).[3] They conclude "not that [the American system of justice] is too lenient, or too severe; [but that] sadly it is both" (p. 252). (Nettler 1979a, p. 44).

Zimring and his colleagues are objecting to a sense of justice that assigns different prices to homicides. The sense of justice to which they object regards the killing of strangers as more serious than the killing of intimates. It also regards killing in the course of committing another crime, usually a robbery, as more serious than killing in the heat of a quarrel between acquaintances or intimates.

---

[3] "This allegation is not accurate since not all homicides in Zimring's sample were charged as murders or priced as such in conviction. A majority of those suspected of killing in the course of committing another felony were convicted of first or second degree murder, but a majority of homicide suspects whose killings were not associated with another felony were convicted of voluntary manslaughter or lesser crimes. Only three percent of 'non-felony murder' suspects were convicted of first degree murder (Zimring et al. 1976, Tables I and V)" (Citation from Nettler 1979a, p. 44, n. 4).

Morality, Once Again

The justice sentiment is a moral one, and morals, as we know, are diverse (Snare 1980). Tests of fair application of laws are adequate only when they include the purposes for which laws allow discretionary application, and these purposes are morally saturated.

From an outsider's point of view, all legal purposes may be challenged and the sense of justice that motivates one tribe or society need not stimulate another. For example, Zimring et al. believe that, with some qualification, a killing is a killing. But this equation fits no known group's sense of justice, as Volume Two, Chapter 5 demonstrated.

Analogy

The present point can be illustrated with a sports analogy. "Fairness" is a ruling which, in games, is termed "a judgment call." There *are* close calls, but in the heat of the contest referees have to make their decisions—"in" or "out," "caught" or "fumbled." And, assuming referees are honest, they make their decisions *according to the rules of the game.*

The rules of the game are not themselves in dispute *within the stadium.* Engaging in the sport includes an agreement to play by its rules. However, *outside the stadium,* one can object to the rules and push for their change. That is, one can ask for a new game.

A similar situation exists when criminologists study the justice of other people. In the Zimring research, Philadelphians' appreciation of the relative "value" of homicides does not regard all killings as equal. Within the "Philly ballpark," unequal judgments are fair if they accord with their rules of the game. Outside that arena, other moralists may criticize Philadelphians' sense of justice, but no facts alter sentiments about which "game" is the better one to play.

An Israeli Example

Mixture of legally relevant factors with a local sense of justice to produce unequal outcomes is illustrated by the differential treatment of youthful offenders in Israel. Rahav (1980) studied responses to juvenile crimes committed by Jews of European descent (Ashkenazim), Jews of Afro-Oriental origin (Sephardim), and Arabs. As expected, punishment varied with the social status of these ethnic groups. European Jews received lighter sentences than Afro-Oriental Jews—after controlling for age, number of siblings, broad categories of instant offense, and number of previous arrests. In addition, Arab youths were more likely to be sent to institutions than Jewish youths.

However, Rahav finds it impossible to account for these unequal results by prejudice. Arab youths are handled by Arab officers who "assign more weight to the social harm caused by the offense, settlement of the issue between the offender's and victim's families, and local public opinion" (Rahav 1980, p. 71). Arab officers, operating with their system of values, are more likely to recommend incarceration for their delinquents than are Jewish official for Jewish delinquents.

The differential treatment of European and Afro-Oriental Jews by Jewish officers is a function of the fact that Sephardic families have poorer resources for controlling their children. Authorities therefore see more of their children as in need of supervision when they commit crimes.

In this example, difference in judicial outcome is not produced by malice, but by the social structure, by the differential adaptability of minorities to that structure, and by differences in minority conceptions of justice.

Summary

In democracies, a people's conception of justice affects how their laws are used. Tests of fair application are adequate only when they include the purposes that allow discretionary application of the law, and these purposes are themselves defined by a sense of justice.

Given this consideration, studies of administration of the criminal law in Western countries in recent years find generally that *legal factors determine decisions far more than do extralegal biases* (Friedman 1975, pp. 172–178, Gottfredson & Gottfredson 1980, Hann et al. 1973, Nettler 1979a).

This finding is more true—it holds with fewer exceptions—as research controls for *complexes* of factors that are legitimately allowed to affect discretion. For example, Don and Michael Gottfredson (1980) survey research on how decisions are produced:

—to report a crime,
—to arrest a suspect,
—to release a suspect before trial,
—to prosecute and, if so, for which crime,
—to sentence, and
—to administer offenders on probation, in institutions, and on parole.

The Gottfredsons conclude that:

> ... from the host of offender, offense, victim, decisionmaker, and situa-
> tional factors that potentially influence individual decisionmaking, three
> appear to play a persistent and major role throughout the system—the
> "seriousness of the offense," the prior criminal conduct of the offender,
> and the personal relationship between the victim of the crime and the
> offender (p. 330).

This summary speaks to the general prevalence of fair application
of the criminal law. However, such generalization carries qualifications. It is qualified (1) by time, place, sex, and race; (2) by individual
differences in lawyers, judges, defendants, and victims; and (3) by extreme cases in which wealth and power produce differential justice.

1. TIME, PLACE, SEX, AND RACE MAY MAKE A DIF-
FERENCE IN APPLICATION OF THE CRIMINAL LAW

Western law has been protective of women and young people. It has
also regarded "the same crime" as more serious when it is committed
by a stranger than when it is committed by an intimate. These orien-
tations toward justice explain, although they may not justify, some
reported differences in responses to crimes committed by women
and by some, but not all, visible minorities.

For example, women appear to be relatively immune to the death
penalty in Canada and the United States. Johnson (1957) reports that
North Carolina sent 660 prisoners to death row between 1909 and
1954, only six of whom were women. Of the women, only two were
executed. Johnson cites chivalry as explanatory and quotes a Carolina governor who, in 1916, commuted the death sentence of a mur-
deress by claiming that, "Humanity does not apply to women the in-
exorable law that it does to men."

Similarly, the Ohio Legislative Service Commission (1961) reports
that, between 1955 and 1958, 50 of the 336 persons charged with first
degree murder were women. But, whereas 31 percent of men were
found guilty when so charged, only eight percent of women were
deemed guilty.

In parallel fashion, research for the Canadian Minister of Justice
(1965) shows that, during the 1950s, 175 men and five women were
sentenced to death. Of these, 71 men (40%) were executed compared with one executed woman (20%).

Time and place make a difference, however. A review of all first
degree murder cases in California from 1958 to 1966 found no differential treatment of the sexes either in verdict or in sentence (Judson
et al. 1969).

Criticism

Unfortunately, many of these studies are flawed. They do not control for all legally relevant variables, case by case, that may legitimately affect disposition. They tell us little or nothing about the careers that preceded the crimes or the circumstances of the last, condemned event. We may infer sexual favoritism from many of these inquiries, but we cannot weigh its importance.

This criticism applies as well to studies of ethnic discrimination in application of the law.

Ethnic Discrepancies

American research has paid especial attention to the possibility that blacks have been unjustly treated by police, judges, and juries. Assessment of fair treatment is complicated by the fact that blacks, when compared with the Caucasoid majority and other minorities, have disproportionately high crime rates and particularly high rates of violent crime (Volume Two, Chapter 3). Assessment is also complicated by changes in race relations in the United States since World War II, with great shifts in the Deep South. Therefore, what may have been true during the first half of this century, and in certain states, may be less true in the latter half. Time and place make a difference.

Early studies found differential responses to black and white serious offenders of such a nature as to suggest prejudice in administration of the law. For example, Garfinkel (1949) noted differences in sentences given to interracial as opposed to intraracial killings in North Carolina during the 1930s and Johnson (1941) recorded similar differences during that decade in Georgia, North Carolina, and Virginia. Independently of one another, these investigators found (a) that blacks who killed whites were more likely to be indicted, convicted, and given the death penalty than whites who killed blacks, and (b) that blacks who killed blacks received lighter sentences than blacks who killed whites.

Similarly, Bullock (1961) reports that Texas gave blacks more punishment than whites for many crimes, even when allowance was made for number of offenders' prior convictions and type of plea entered. He notes a reversal of this tendency in the lighter sentences given blacks for murder and he suggests, but does not demonstrate, that this may be a function of most homicides having been intraracial.

As with tests of sexual favoritism, these studies are also defective in the poor controls they employ to describe the kinds of crime, criminal, and victim. "Homicide," for example, is not one type of activity.. But these studies tend to bracket first degree murder with second degree murder and manslaughter. In criticism of Johnson's research, Green (1964, p. 349) points out that the percentage of cases of "first degree murder is substantially the highest for N-W [Negro-White combination of offender-victim], much lower for the W-W, and by far the lowest for the N-N."

A different picture of judicial fairness is provided by the Stanford study of first degree murder trials in California (Judson et al. 1969). This review not only found no sex discrimination in application of the law, but it also found no ethnic differentials among defendants who were black, white, or of Mexican ancestry. Furthermore, it found no difference in the disposition of whites who killed blacks or of blacks who killed whites. The death penalty in California was applied more frequently to offenders with criminal careers and, to a lesser extent, to those who had actively resisted arrest or who offered an insanity plea.

Gibson's (1978) study of the sentencing of felons in Fulton County (principally Atlanta), Georgia, parallels the California findings. His analysis of the disposition of 1,219 cases by 11 judges reveals no evidence of racial differentiation in type of sentence or length of sentence when controls are employed for seriousness of charge and previous felony convictions. However, individual judges vary so that "blacks are the victims of discrimination by some judges, but the beneficiaries of discrimination by others" (p. 470).

In similar vein, Green's (1964) study of the handling of 118 robbery indictments and 291 burglary cases in a Philadelphia court finds that, when controls are applied for gravity of criminal career and gravity of instant offense, the charge of racial prejudice fails. Sentences vary most dramatically with offenders' prior records.

Green's study provides a caution for other research that would test for ethnic discrimination in sentencing. He observes that "robbery" is not the same kind of event when predator and victim are black-white or white-white as opposed to black-black. The first two kinds of attack exhibit "a much higher degree of malicious intent." Similarly, black-white and white-white "burglaries" are not of the same calibre as black-black thefts. The former tend to be more serious.

Additional Qualifiers

Thomson and Zingraff (1981) add to research on this topic by noting, as we have, that dispositions vary with cultural and jurisdictional contexts. These investigators tested fairness of sentences given all males convicted of armed robbery in a southeastern state during 1969, 1973, and 1977. They divided sentence length into "least severe, moderately severe, and most severe" by taking as a categorizing instrument half the standard deviation above and below mean sentence length for each year. They then weighed contributions of selected legal and extralegal variables upon sentence length. The legal "causes" of sentence severity were presence or absence of a previous incarceration and number of previous sentences, dichotomized as one or two or more. These indicators are *not,* of course, measures of total prior record or of all legally relevant considerations.

The extralegal influences assessed were race, years of schooling, and occupation. They find that:

> In 1977 whites incarcerated for armed robbery had a greater than average chance of receiving the least severe sentence, while nonwhites had a greater than average chance of receiving a moderately severe sentence. Members of each racial group had average chances of receiving the most severe sentence. Persons with a prior incarceration had a greater than average chance of receiving the most severe sentence and a less than average chance of receiving either the least severe or a moderate sentence. Prior incarceration is evidently more influential than race in the determination of sentence length, as evidenced by the size of the coefficients and by the fact that with all years combined prior incarceration alone remained significant (p. 875).

More Detailed Research

Konečni and Ebbesen (1982) report a more detailed procedure for coding events leading to sentences for felonies in San Diego County Superior Court. Almost 100 trained coders worked for two years classifying several hundred items in about 1,200 court files, 1976–1977. For example, they recorded:

- demographic characteristics of offenders
- prior record of defendants
- their employment and social history
- their medical, psychological, and psychiatric evaluations
- charges upon arrest
- charges upon conviction
- court-related data such as bail, custody, and plea-bargaining
- characteristics of the crime
- evidence from witnesses and physical circumstances
- content of defendant's statement, including degree of apparent premeditation, remorse, admission of guilt
- probation officer's assessment
- probation officer's recommendation
- details of the sentence

These many "independent variables" were then tested for their relationship to four possible outcomes: State prison sentence, county jail sentence (almost always followed by a probationary order), straight probation (without incarceration), and all other outcomes such as commitment to a mental hospital or fine without incarceration or probation.

Of all the possible determinants of sentence, only four were significantly correlated with quality of sentence:

1. Type of crime.
2. Offender's prior record.
3. Offender's status between arrest and conviction (Released on own recognizance; released on bail; held in jail, then released on bail; held in jail throughout).
4. Probation officer's sentence recommendation [p. 308].

Contrary to some of the findings of sociopsychological research with simulated cases and some of the findings from other times and places, Konečni and Ebbesen discovered *no effects* upon sentence of offender's physical attractiveness, age, sex, race, education, marital status, or religion—when prior record and severity of crime were controlled. Nor did they find any "judge effects." Individual differences among judges that lead to reputations of "softies" and "hanging judges" reflect two facts in this jurisdiction: That "different judges . . . are consistently assigned different kinds of cases" and "the way probation officers varied the rate of prison and straight-probation recommendations across judges" (p. 316).

Statistical modeling of the data indicates that "judges' sentencing decisions are caused by probation officers' recommendations, which are, in turn, caused by the three case factors . . . severity of the crime, prior record, and jail/bail status" (pp. 320–321). The researchers conclude:

> . . . probation officers' recommendations—the key cause of judges' sentencing decisions—were influenced by severity of the crime, prior record, jail/bail status, and two interactions according to which the effect of prior record was substantially augmented by the higher levels of severity of the crime and jail/bail status [p. 322].

Incidental Findings

This large-scale investigation "spun off" some additional results of interest. In keeping with our thesis that "reasons may not be causes" (Volume One, Chapter 2), Konečni and Ebbesen note that judges, and others involved in the sentencing process, believe their decisions reflect complex cognitive processes whereas research shows that "very few factors influence sentencing decisions, and so in this sense the decisions appear to be quite simple." (p. 325). The authors add:

> The fact that judges *talk* about numerous factors (as in the simulations) may have nothing to do with the causal factors that control their decisions. One must not confuse their possibly quite complex thought processes with the quite simple causes of their behavior [p. 325, emphasis in the original].

Summary

Much research on this issue has suffered from crude categories of crimes studied and inadequate attention to coding of the legally permissible considerations in sentencing. More recent American and Canadian studies, with better controls, find little evidence that ethnicity of the accused or ethnicities of predator and victim account for much of the differential outcomes in responding to crime and delinquency (Bernstein et al. 1977, Chiricos & Waldo 1975, Cohen & Kluegel 1978, Hagan 1974a, 1974b, Konečni & Ebbesen 1982). However, exceptions to this generalization may occur in responses to forcible rape and homicide in selected regions.

Differential Responses to Forcible Rape and Homicide

Forcible rape and homicide have been the two principal categories of crime for which the death sentence has been given. Challenges to the legality of capital punishment have alleged that this extreme sanction has been applied in discriminatory fashion.

In Canada, for example, a disproportionate number of French Canadians have been executed, but Canadian Indians have been more successful than prisoners of other ethnicity in appeals against the death sentence (Chandler et al. 1976). Research is so thin, however, that no conclusion can be drawn about fair administration of this sentence in Canada.

A more plausible charge of unfair application of the law occurs when one compares death sentences meted out to American blacks and whites for forcible rape and homicide.

The Wolfgang-Riedel Study

Wolfgang and Riedel (1973, 1976, 1977), with the help of many research associates, conducted an investigation of sentencing practices that has been cited in Congressional and judicial hearings and by numerous textbooks. This research analyzed American executions for forcible rape from 1945 to 1965. Although 18 states allowed the death penalty for this crime during some portion of the study period, only 12 states are said by the investigators to have executed "substantial numbers," unspecified, for this crime.

Data collection began for these 12 states, but Maryland was omitted from final analysis because of deadline pressure. Information on more than 3,000 rape convictions in 250 counties of 11 southern states was processed with inspection of 44 variables that might conceivably have influenced disposition. Some of these variables are legally relevant, and some not, but measures of many of the important factors are skimpy. In particular, details of the prior records of offenders are lacking. In addition, tests of the impact of legal and extra-legal attributes were conducted *one variable at a time.* Since judge and jury operate with a *patterned* conception of the criminal event, weighing *one* possible determinant of sentence, separate from a combination of factors, is not an appropriate procedure. It allows no assessment of the *power* of a "significant variable" to produce its alleged effect upon judicial decision.

Nevertheless, Wolfgang and Riedel (1976, p. 110) report that, "for purposes of submitting testimony in litigation conducted by the [NAACP's] Legal Defense Fund," the data base was reduced to seven states. However, the data base is further restricted when relationships are studied between race and sentence, between the four possible racial combinations of culprit and victim (N-N, N-W, W-W, W-N), and between racial pairings, commission of a concurrent crime, and sentence. Only five states contribute data about the connection between race and sentence. Furthermore, when racial pairings of predator and victim are examined, the tables are compressed so that black convict-white victim attacks are compared with *all other racial pairings combined.* In addition, the important tables for racial pairings are sometimes drawn for six states (1976, p. 111, Table 2) and, sometimes, as when the control variable of "contemporaneous offense" is included, for only three states (1976, pp. 113–114, Tables 5, 6, 7).

Wolfgang and Riedel report that blacks who raped white women were far more likely to have been executed than white rapists or than blacks who raped black women. However, scholars who cite this finding say, confusingly, that it applies to 11 states (Bowers & Pierce 1980, p. 582; Dorin 1981, pp. 1669, 1682; Hagan 1977c, p. 134), seven states (Clarke & Koch 1976, p. 63; Wolfgang 1974, p. 242, Wolfgang & Riedel 1976, p. 118; 1977, p. 125), and six states (Bowers 1974, p. 79). No author refers to the analysis for only *three* states when the significant control for concurrent offense is employed.

This point is important because, while the general conclusion is plausible, the *degree of association* between variables can increase or decrease with changes in the size of the data base (Tufte 1974, pp. 78–81).

Wolfgang and Riedel (1976) recalculated information from one state, Georgia, with a statistic that allowed them to control several variables at a time and they find again that black men who raped white women were more likely to have received the death sentence than other rapists. But they add that more recent offenders are not sentenced to death.

Caution

The history of "racial etiquette" in the United States, particularly prior to the 1960s, makes the Wolfgang-Riedel conclusion believable. Unfortunately, their mode of analyzing data does not make it possible to test competing hypotheses, hypotheses which lawyers for the accused Southern states might want to advance.

Whether or not we prefer other interpretations, they remain hypotheses which scientists must entertain if their inferences are to be fair. In particular, the very history of race relations that makes it plausible that black men who raped white women were more severely punished than other rapists also suggests the possibility that such rapists in the Deep South may have differed in legally admissible qualities—in short, that they may have been a different kind of offender.

In accord with Green's findings about differences between intra- and inter-racial burglary and robbery, and with the sense of justice that regards attacks by strangers as more serious than attacks by intimates, the judged quality of crime can vary with the social distance of predators and victims.

"Rape" is no more one kind of crime than is "burglary," "robbery," or "murder." Roman Polanski's (1981) film, "Tess," makes the point: Was Tess D'Urberville "raped" or just "seduced"?

LaFree's Study

The point applies as well to a recent study of the judicial processing of 881 suspects charged with "forcible sex offenses" between 1970 and 1975 in a midwestern metropolis (LaFree 1980).

The author titles his report, "official reactions to rape," but the crimes charged included "rape, armed rape, sodomy, armed sodomy, assault and battery with intent to rape, and assault and battery with intent to gratify," and excluded statutory rape and male victims (p.

844, fn. 2). LaFree notes that "kidnapping was frequently included with charges for forcible sex offenses," but he drops this aspect of the crime from his analysis. He then controls for race, defendant's age and prior criminal record, preference of victim to prosecute, presence of witnesses, use of weapons, and whether the crime was "attempted sexual assault" or "sexual assault."

LaFree's step-by-step analysis of the processing of defendants by racial pairings (there were no white defendants accused of raping black women) finds that:

> Compared to other defendants, black men who assaulted white women received (1) more serious charges and (2) longer sentences, and were more likely to (3) have their cases filed as felonies, (4) receive executed sentences, and (5) be incarcerated in the state penitentiary. At the same time, black men who assaulted white women were no more likely than other suspects to be arrested or found guilty (p. 842).

These findings may be true, but their interpretation is clouded by the crude categorization of each crime as either "attempted sexual assault" or "sexual assault," by failure to control for concurrent crimes, and by failure to control for degree of acquaintance between offender and victim. In short, the *quality* of these crimes is poorly described, and quality may vary with different pairings of blacks and whites, strangers and acquaintances.

Academic Argument

Arguments about fair application of the death sentence in rape cases are now academic in the United States since the Supreme Court declared in *Coker* v. *Georgia* (1977) that the rape of an adult female was not a capital crime. However, arguments will continue about the fair application of lesser sentences for this offense.

Events and Their Meanings

We have noted repeatedly that attributions of responsibility for crimes vary with moral judgments about actors and their circumstances. Both laboratory experiments and field studies demonstrate this variation. It is a variation that assigns different meanings to apparently similar physical events.

A popular hypothesis acknowledges this and holds that condemnation of a predator diminishes if his or her action occurs in social settings that tolerate such behavior or, at least, that accord it lesser significance. Martha Myers (1980b) phrases the assumption this way:

Responsibility of the actor is diminished if the social setting, in the form
of subcultural values and norms, tolerates the action. This expectation
applies specifically to criminal action involving black victims and offenders. Here, attributors may diminish the actor's responsibility because
they consider the act situationally (i.e., subculturally) determined rather
than internally caused, and because they do not expect blacks to conform
to middle class norms (p. 407).

Myers tested this assumption on a sample of felony defendants in
Marion County (Indianapolis), Indiana, between 1970 and 1976. She
found that, for 130 cases of "sexual assault":

... jurors were more likely to convict if the defendant had prior convictions or had been identified by eyewitnesses. They were less likely to
convict if the defendant was black and had victimized a black. For other
crimes, jurors did not base their verdicts on these variables (p. 414).

Reprise

Research has not given us a description of sexual attacks that permits a judgment about the homogeneity of events called "rape."
Without a depiction of racial pairings and relevant circumstances case
by case, the possibility cannot be tested that qualities of crimes may
vary with different racial combinations. We are left with statistical
manipulation of aggregate data that may obscure the *pattern* of considerations that produced differential sentencing.

This criticism is not intended to reduce vigilance against unfair
treatment of ethnic groups or social classes. It is intended to alert us
to possible deficiencies of research that would inform social policy
with low-grade data. This caution applies as well to studies of racial
discrimination in response to murder.

Differential Sentencing for Murder

Bowers and Pierce (1980) bring together an impressive array of
data to demonstrate that racial prejudice affects all stages of legal response to murder suspects—from the laying of charges to indictments, convictions, and death sentences.

Their research was stimulated by the attempts of some states to re-
tain the death penalty after the United States Supreme Court, in a 5 to
4 decision in *Furman* v. *Georgia* (1972), held that capital punishment, as then administered, was unconstitutional. Some states re-
acted by attempting either to eliminate judicial discretion in capital
cases through a mandatory death penalty or by establishing "guided
discretion" statutes. The Supreme Court later held (in *Gregg* v.

Table 2.1 Probability of Receiving the Death Sentence in Florida, Georgia, Texas, and Ohio for Criminal Homicide, by Race of Offender and Victim (from effective dates of respective post-Furman capital statutes through 1977)*

Offender/ Victim Racial Combinations	(1) Estimated Number of Offenders	(2) Persons Sentenced to Death	(3) Overall Probability of Death Sentence
Florida			
Black kills white	240	53	.221
White kills white	1768	82	.046
Black kills black	1922	12	.006
White kills black	80	0	.000
Georgia			
Black kills white	258	43	.167
White kills white	1006	42	.042
Black kills black	2458	12	.005
White kills black	71	2	.028
Texas			
Black kills white	344	30	.087
White kills white	3616	56	.015
Black kills black	2597	2	.001
White kills black	143	1	.007
Ohio			
Black kills white	173	44	.254
White kills white	803	37	.046
Black kills black	1170	20	.017
White kills black	47	0	.000

*Reprinted, with permission of the National Council on Crime and Delinquency, from William J. Bowers and Glenn L. Pierce, "Arbitrariness and Discrimination under Post-Furman Statutes," *Crime & Delinquency,* October 1980, pp. 594, 599.

Georgia and related cases, 1976) that the mandatory death penalty was invalid because it eliminated discretion and might cause juries to decide guilt, not from the evidence before them, but from the sentence to follow their findings.

Some states then continued to apply the death penalty under revised laws that "guided" discretion and Bowers and Pierce were interested in testing for racial bias in the application of these "post-Furman" statutes. They analyzed all death sentences for the five years between 1972 and 1977 inclusive in Florida, Georgia, Ohio, and Texas. These four states handed down approximately 70 percent of the capital penalities in the United States during this period. However, Ohio has since rescinded its death penalty law but, as of the first months of 1981, 35 states and the federal government maintain the death penalty.

Bowers and Pierce find that white offenders are more likely than black offenders to receive the death penalty in three of the four states surveyed. However, when murders are tallied by racial pairings of convict and victim, a constistent pattern is revealed: Blacks who kill whites are more frequently sentenced to death in all four states than any of the other three pairings by race of murderer and victim. Table 2.1 provides the numbers and differential probabilities.

Some of the facts of this table can be summarized as follows:

1. A black person in Florida convicted of killing a white person has about 37 times the likelihood of being sentenced to death as a black individual who kills another black person.

2. In Texas, black offenders with white victims are 87 times more likely to receive the death penalty than are blacks who kill other blacks. A black in Texas who kills a white has 5.8 times the chance of being sentenced to death than does a white who kills another white.

Furthermore, these differences persist even when the murders are classified as "felony" and "non-felony," a classification which Bowers and Pierce hold is itself subject to prosecutors' prejudice. Table 2.2 reveals the persistent differential probabilities of the death sentence with the four possible racial pairings of offender and victim.

Bowers and Pierce also report, but they do not tabulate, the possibility that controlling for such aggravating circumstances as victim vulnerability, multiple offenders or victims, and degree of preparation for the crime do not change this discriminatory pattern of sentencing. Unfortunately, the investigators do not control for three significant, legally allowable circumstances considered to make murder more serious: Previous acquaintance of offender and victim, aggravated battery or mutilation, and, most important, offenders' prior record.

Nevertheless, Bowers and Pierce conclude from these data, and from evidence of disparities between jurisdictions within states and between police reports of homicidal circumstances and prosecutors' charges, that prejudice is so pervasive that the death penalty cannot be imposed without arbitrariness and discrimination. They admit that a people's sense of justice may *interpret* black murders of whites as

Table 2.2 Probability of Receiving the Death Sentence in Florida, Georgia, and Texas for Felony and Nonfelony Murder, by Race of Offender and Victim (from effective dates of respective post-Furman capital statutes through 1977) *

Offender/ Victim Racial Combinations	Felony-Type Murder			Nonfelony-Type Murder		
	(1) Estimated Number of Offenders	*(2)* Persons Sentenced to Death	*(3)* Probability of Death Sentence	*(1)* Estimated Number of Offenders	*(2)* Persons Sentenced to Death	*(3)* Overall Probability of Death Sentence
Florida						
Black kills white	143	46	.323	97	7	.072
White kills white	303	65	.215	1465	17	.012
Black kills black	160	7	.044	1762	5	.003
White kills black	11	0	.000	69	0	.000
Georgia						
Black kills white	134	39	.291	124	3	.024
White kills white	183	37	.202	823	6	.007
Black kills black	205	8	.039	2253	4	.002
White kills black	13	2	.154	58	0	.000
Texas						
Black kills white	173	28	.162	171	2	.012
White kills white	378	48	.127	3238	8	.002
Black kills black	121	2	.017	2476	0	.000
White kills black	30	1	.033	113	0	.000

*Reproduced from W.J. Bowers and G.L. Pierce. 1980. "Arbitrariness and discrimination under post-*Furman* capital statutes." Crime & Delinq., 26:563–635. © 1980 by The National Council on Crime and Delinquency and reprinted with its permission.

more serious than other racial pairings in homicide, but they attribute this sense of outrage to prejudice and a history of racial subjugation. They write:

> This is not to say that killings of whites and killings by blacks will not seem more vile and heinous to most people. Where there is animosity, prejudice, and stereotyping along racial lines—resulting, perhaps, from long-standing patterns of discrimination and deeply rooted racial attitudes and fears—people will be more shocked and outraged by crimes that victimize members of the dominant racial group, by crimes that are perpetrated by members of the subjugated or subordinated racial group, and especially by killings in which a minority group offender crosses racial boundaries to murder a majority group victim (pp. 630-631).

Historical Possibility and Research Sensitivity

The sad history of American race relations, and of ethnic conflict universally, make it plausible that people of diverse cultures have difficulty liking one another and that people who dislike one another have trouble doing justice to objects of their contempt.

No thermometer is available with which to gauge the "fever of ethnicity," as Alpert (1972) calls it. Most measures of racial attitudes are reactive, distorted by the transparency of their intention and contaminated with the "social desirability" factor (Edwards 1957). However, such unobtrusive measures suggest that blacks and whites do not like each other very much and do not trust one another, and this seems as true in Canada and the Caribbean as it is in the United States and South Africa (Lambley 1981).

"Proxemic" studies[4] in classrooms and on schoolgrounds (Crooks 1970, Lundberg & Dickson 1952), observations of personal relations in mixed neighborhoods and at mixed parties (Guest & Zuiches 1977, Molotch 1969, Wilkins 1981), and studies of patterns of residence reveal integration[5] to be less common than separation (Coleman & Kelly 1976, Darroch & Marston 1977, deLeeuw et al. 1976, Fly & Reinhart 1980, Frey 1979, Levine & Meyer 1977, Rossell et al. 1978, Van Valey et al. 1977). The separation and hostility are even more apparent, of course, within the confines of American prisons (Ramsey 1976). The black anthropologist Gwaltney (1980) concludes that, "Every reasonable black person thinks that most white people do not mean him well."

Gwaltney has a point. His point gains substance from mock jury trials in which white citizens are asked to "sentence" imaginary black and white rapists whose victims are variously black or white women. Feild (1979) conducted such an experiment with 896 adults, evenly divided between men and women, in an American town. With stories of rape incidents, Feild manipulated race and physical attractiveness of the victim, her sexual experience, race of the defendant, strength of evidence, and whether the rape was, or was not, "victim-precipitated." However, he omitted the variable of prior acquaintance. Nevertheless, Feild found that his white "jurors" treated black and white rapists similarly when their victims were black women, but that they dealt more harshly with black attackers of white

[4] "Proxemics" is a neologism referring to the study of how people space themselves (Hall 1959, 1974, Sommer 1969). Proxemics involves forms of sociometric that can be unobtrusively employed to tally who associates with (likes) whom.

[5] Many writers confuse the "congregation" of groups with their "integration." To integrate means to unify—to make a new unit out of disparate entities. To congregate means to gather together, from the Latin root (*grex*), a flock or herd. People, and other animals, can congregate—voluntarily or. under coercion—*without* integrating.

women. The correlation is low, indicating that the race effect is minimal, yet it is there.

Against the backdrop of American history, it seems reasonable to conclude from such research that white judges and juries may have difficulty doing justice to black defendants who breach the racial barrier in violent attacks. Acknowledgement of this difficulty does not constitute evidence of the actual operation of bias in a judicial setting, but it justifies continuing research with improved observational techniques.

2. INDIVIDUAL VARIATIONS AMONG LAWYERS, JUDGES, JURIES, DEFENDANTS, AND VICTIMS PRODUCE DIFFERENTIAL RESPONSES TO CRIME.

It is commonly assumed that the people who plead cases, and who hear them, vary in attitudes and abilities. It is also assumed, with support from socio-psychological experimentation, that we judge people we like differently from those we dislike. These assumptions are undeniable, yet what they mean for the administration of criminal law is unclear.

On an anecdotal level it is easy to point to unjust disparities in the treatment of suspects. The former director of the U.S. federal prison system, James V. Bennett (1964), told a Senate committee:

> That some judges are arbitrary and even sadistic in their sentencing practices is notoriously a matter of record. By reason of senility or a virtually pathological emotional complex some judges summarily impose the maximum on defendants convicted of certain types of crimes or all types of crimes. . . . There is one judge who, as a matter of routine, always gives the maximum sentence and who of course is avoided by every defense lawyer. If they have the misfortune of having their case arise before him they lay the ground for appeals since experience has indicated the appeals court is sympathetic and will, if possible, overturn the sentencing court. I know of one judge who continued to sit on the bench and sentence defendants to prison while he was undergoing shock treatments for a mental illness (p. 311).

Bennett goes on to describe the kinds of sentence disparity that are a perennial source of convict complaint: One judge gives a first offender 15 years for passing a bad check for $58.40 while, in a parallel case, another judge gives a man with two previous misdemeanor convictions 30 days for passing a bad check for $35.20. A middle-aged treasurer of a credit union serves 117 days for embezzling $24,000 to cover his gambling debts while another embezzler of like age, but with a more honorable record, serves 20 years for a similar theft. Bennett comments on the injustices of:

> . . . a war veteran, a 39-year-old attorney who has never been in trouble before, serving 11 years for illegally importing parrots into this country. Another [in] the same institution is a middle-aged tax accountant who on tax fraud charges received 31 years and 31 days in consecutive sentences. In stark contrast, at the same institution . . . an unstable young man served out his 98-day sentence for armed bank robbery (p. 331).

The fact of sentence disparity has led to a search for its sources in the attitudes of judges and juries, in the skills of attorneys, and in attributes of defendants, witnesses, and victims. Research on this topic is voluminous and only a brief summary of findings can be presented here:

1. "Formal" (more legalistic) judges, as opposed to those who operate with a broader concept of justice, tend to be more legally restrained and to accord more importance to the seriousness of the crime they are trying.

John Hagan (1975c) tested the impact of "law and order" attitudes on the handling of criminal cases in Alberta in 1973. He found that among 36 judges the most important determinant of length of sentence handed down was gravity of the offense charged. Prior convictions were second in importance, and no significant effect was found for race of the defendant or number of concurrent charges. However, when judges were divided as "high" or "low" on Hagan's "law and order" scale, the more legalistic judges continued to sentence by offense gravity, but the less legalistic judges were more influenced by the defendant's race and number of current charges. The less formal judges treated Indians and Metis more leniently. Whether such unequal treatment is fair or unfair depends, again, on one's sense of justice.

2. Judges' personal characteristics—their age, ethnicity, political party affiliation, religion, and socioeconomic background—may interact with legally relevant considerations as they decide cases, but the contribution of these possible biasing factors to decision is slight.

Early studies of the social backgrounds and ethicopolitical preferences of judges suffer from the same defects discussed in relation to the sentencing of classes of defendant: They have looked at possible biasing variables one at a time rather than assessing the *complex* of legally relevant and irrelevant factors as they interact with qualities of the cases being judged. In short, early studies report correlations without being able to assign them causal weights in the production of decisions. For example, Nagel (1965) analyzed decisions of 298 judges serving in state courts of last appeal and in the U.S. Supreme Court. He categorized decisions among 15 types of legal suit and assigned "decision scores" to each judge. Some significant associations appear between political party affiliation and judgment. Nagel reports a tendency for Democratic judges:

> to favor defendants in criminal cases;
> to favor administrative agencies against businesses;
> to favor the claimant in unemployment compensation cases;
> to find a constitutional violation in the conduct of criminal cases;
> to favor the government in tax suits;
> to favor the tenant in landlord-tenant disputes;
> to favor the consumer in sales suits;
> to favor the injured party in motor vehicle accident cases; and
> to favor the employee in employee injury cases.

In a similar study, Gibson (1978) found a slight tendency among 11 Georgia judges for older judges who are "fundamentalist Protestants" with strong ties to the community to sentence blacks more severely than do their colleagues.

These are interesting correlations, but they do not tell us how much weight, if any, personal attributes and political preferences bear upon judicial decision. In research that attempts to measure this, Bowen (1965) tested the importance of social characteristics for judicial disposition among state and appellate judges. He found correlations similar to those reported by Nagel and others, but his multiple regression analysis shows that none of the variables "significantly correlated" with judicial decision accounted for much of the variation among judges. Age and party preference were the most reliable markers of personal bias, but no single social characteristic "explained" more than 16 percent of the differences in decisions. When Bowen combined six personal factors in test of their contribution to judgment, they accounted for less than 30 percent of the variance in all kinds of cases except one.

In keeping with Bowen's conclusion, Walker (1972) found no influence of judges' political preference upon 1,117 decisions in civil liberties litigation.

3. The title given a crime sometimes changes judgment of it.

Research on this possibility is thin. It suggests, however, that some differences in sentence may be produced by nature of the charge rather than by nature of the crime. For example, Shea (1974) had 100 British magistrates in 13 jurisdictions assign hypothetical sentences to descriptions of a motoring offense and a public brawl. He found that when the same operator's offense was charged as "careless driving," rather than "dangerous driving," it produced a difference in likely sentence. However, calling the brawl a "riot," as opposed to an "affray and unlawful assembly," produced no difference in sentence.

4. Poverty may make a difference in the justice one receives.

Nagel's (1965) study reports that indigent defendants in assault and larceny cases are less likely than non-indigent persons to have a preliminary hearing, to be tried promptly, to receive bail, to be awarded probation, and to be acquitted. However, when found guilty, non-indigent defendants are given longer sentences.

These findings are unfortunately obscured by poor controls for quality of crimes.

5. The relative attractiveness of defendant and victim may influence verdicts.

For obvious reasons, no test of this hypothesis has been conducted in actual trials. However, criminal lawyers assume this possibility and sociopsychological experiments support it.

A defense attorney's common tactic is to make the victim appear as a "low-life" who deserved whatever damage s(he) suffered. The prominent defender, Percy Foreman, is quoted as saying that, "The best defense in a murder case is the fact that the deceased should have been killed regardless of how it happened" (Smith 1966).

Simulated jury experiments demonstrate that "the same crime" is judged differently depending on how victims and their predators appear. Unappealing defendants draw more severe penalties than do "worthy" defendants. Mock juries are less certain of the guilt of good-looking defendants than of ugly ones and they tend to assign lighter punishment to attractive defendants (Efran 1974). Conversely, attractive victims stimulate more severe penalties against their predators than do unattractive ones (Landy & Aronson 1969). In simulated personal injury trials, "juries" tend more frequently to award favorable judgments, and larger ones, to attractive plaintiffs (Stephan & Tully 1977). Beauty is one form of power.

In addition, mock jurors evaluate similar defendants differently when they appear in prison garb or personal dress, and when they appear under armed supervision or without it. Accused individuals who appear in personal dress *with* armed guard or in prison uniform *without* armed guard are judge more harshly. However, an unexpected "sympathy effect" is produced—at least among university students—for accused persons who appear in prison uniform under armed supervision (Fontaine & Kiger 1978).

It must be remembered that these are *simulations* of real-life jury work. In keeping with Konečni and Ebbesen's research (p. 40), there.

may be discrepancies between the opinions of artificial juries and real ones, and between juries and judges.

6. Judges tend to sentence more harshly those defendants who opt for trial by jury.

In a report aptly titled, "He takes some of my time; I take some of his," Uhlman and Walker (1980) analyze 29,000 felony cases in an urban American court and show that:

> jury defendants are punished with substantially greater harshness than are plea and bench convictees in essentially similar criminal cases. Regardless of sentencing philosophy, virtually every judge who sentenced jury, bench, and plea defendants sentenced jury defendants far more harshly and sent them to jail more frequently. Stiffer penalties for jury defendants appears to be the operational, though unstated, judicial policy, exercised out of the apparent administrative interest in reducing the number of lengthy jury trials (p. 323).

Nagel (1965) reports a similar possibility from his analysis of 846 felonious assault cases and 1,103 grand larceny cases in American state jurisdictions and 196 assault trials and 785 interstate larceny trials in federal courts. He finds that seeking a jury trial is likely to result in a denial of probation when the defendant is found guilty. However, Nagel correctly notes that:

> The relation between jury trial and probation denial may represent a penalty for having sought an expensive jury trial or it may reflect the possibility that more severe larceny and assault cases are tried by juries (p. 8).

Adequate control for severity of "similar crime" has yet to be exercised in studies testing for disadvantage of defendants before juries.

7. In deciding guilt or innocence, juries tend to be more lenient than judges.

Kalven and Zeisel (1966) compared the evaluations by 555 judges of 3,576 criminal cases decided by juries. They found that juries, compared with judges, tend to sympathize with youth and old age, with physical handicap, with war veterans, and with women-mothers-widows. Jurors are also more moved by defendants who are attractive and repentant. Repentant defendants with family responsibilities are particularly likely to stimulate jury sympathy. In one case a judge noted:

> Jury of eleven women, one man; very sympathetic to defendant's wife. Lovely woman, impressed jury. . . . Tears came to wife's eyes on witness stand and four of the jurors cried with her (p. 292).

Judges perceive what moves jurors, but they yield less often to these emotional considerations.

In the Kalven-Zeisel study, judges and juries agreed on conviction or acquittal in about 75 percent of the cases. When they disagreed, juries tended to be more lenient; judges were more likely to convict.

A similar finding comes out of the Chicago Jury Project (Broader 1959) that examined 1,500 criminal cases. Although judge and jury agreed on verdicts in 81 percent of the cases, when they disagreed, judges were much more likely to convict.

Judges and juries disagree most about interpretation of evidence. They disagree secondarily because they have different attitudes toward some laws. Jurors are more likely to regard selected laws as unfair. Judges and juries also disagree because they sometimes have different facts with which to work, judges being better informed.

8. Jury size and voting rules produce differences in verdicts.

Roper (1980) compared the work of 110 American juries composed of nearly 1,000 jurors and found that twelve members disagree ("hang the jury") more often than do six members. Experimental research confirms this (Padawer-Singer & Barton 1975).

However, a six-person jury produces more errors than does a twelve-person jury and it is less likely to represent the population from which it is drawn (Penrod & Hastie 1979, pp. 469, 482).

The smaller the size of the jury and the lower the quorum requirements, the more likely is the jury to reach a verdict on its first ballot (Penrod & Hastie 1979, p. 467).

Furthermore, if a defendant is guilty, s(he) will do better with larger juries using a unanimous decision rule. Such panels are less likely to convict on first ballot (Penrod & Hastie 1979, p. 468).

9. Politically conservative jurors of higher socioeconomic status are more likely than others to adhere to the rules of procedure and be guided by the evidence.

Reed and Reed (1977) tested this hypothesis among 103 jurors in a small southern city. Cluster analysis of juror attributes indicated that politically conservative jurors of higher social status behaved:

> . . . more in harmony with the legal ideal. . . . They saw jury service as a duty, thought the venire should be a cross-section of the community, tended to vote the evidence in the case rather than extraneous matter, and reached their verdict after deliberation. Their voting behavior, however, was strongly in favor of the state in criminal cases and the defendant in civil cases (p. 84).

Blum (1980) speaks to this issue in noting that complex legal suits—civil and criminal—tend to be beyond the competence of representative juries. This applies with greater force to judgment of high-echelon "white-collar crimes"—those involving tangled financial affairs. In illustration, the jury foreman in the IBM-Memorex case told the judge:

> If you can find a jury that's both a computer technician, a lawyer, and economist—knows all about that stuff—yes, I think you could have a qualified jury, but we don't know anything about that (Blum 1980, p. 1).

Blum draws an axiom: "The longer the trial is expected to last, the less qualified the jury is likely to be."

Legal complexity reveals yet another conflict in attempts to do justice: The ideal of well-informed, dispassionate, and logical juries conflicts with the ideal of democratic representation.

Suggestions

Discretion is an unavoidable feature of decision (Wexler 1975). By its nature, discretion is subject to abuse, but attempts to achieve perfect justice by eliminating or controlling discretion produce other abuses. From ancient times to the present, it has been recognized that "Rigorous law is often rigorous injury" (Terence ca. 165 B.C.) and that "Absolute justice denies freedom" (Camus 1955).

Efforts to reduce sentence disparities seek a middle course between inflexible rules and flaccid dispositions. They include suggestions such as these:

1. That legal aid be assured all defendants.

2. That periodic "sentencing institutes" be convened at which judges receive "refresher courses" and instruction from "experts" in forensic studies.

3. That "sentencing councils" displace judges and juries. Years ago Sheldon Glueck (1936) proposed that sentences be devised by a three-person panel composed of a judge, psychiatrist or psychologist, and a sociologist or educator.

4. That a permanent government agency be established to review periodically the status of judicial work and to make recommendations to legislators. Both private and public organizations now engage in this work.

5. That the information now processed in simple fashion by probation officers and judges, but given a complex coloration, be computerized. Konecni and Ebbesen (1982) write:

> . . . arguments for keeping judges in the sentencing process seem weak. Some of the counterarguments we used emphasize the importance of

keeping solid data within the legal system, and . . . suggest that the sentencing process could be considerably improved by computerization. Computer-based decisions, especially sentences, are of course, anathema to judges and other people in legal circles. . . . The fact of the matter is that the causal model of sentencing is so simple and straightforward that not just judges but also probation officers could be replaced by a very simple computer program that would take severity of the crime, prior record, and jail/bail status into accounts—if the objective were simply to mimic what is presently being done. After all, severity of the crime, prior record, and what appears to be the major cause of variation in jail/bail status—the arrest charges—are all straightforward bits of information, known long before the conviction; in fact, they are known immediately after the arrest! [p. 329, emphasis theirs].

6. That bail be eliminated or, lacking this, that it be administered by clerks of the court, as it is in Kentucky, rather than by brokers (bondsmen) who profit from, and sometimes corrupt, the present system.

Each of these recommendations may appeal to someone without satisfying everyone's sense of justice. Their cost-effectiveness is another matter. When we try to achieve mixed objectives, and conflicting objectives, with limited knowledge, we can only approximate the complicated ideal of justice. We never attain perfect justice.

3. WEALTH AND POWER SOMETIMES PRODUCE DIFFERENTIAL JUSTICE

Power qualifies justice. Power is not all of one kind, of course, and there are contexts in which it distorts justice. Power works by keeping private what might ordinarily be public, by economic reprisal and political threat, and by outright purchase of a warping of the law. Examples are legion.

Large corporations and government agencies seem reluctant to prosecute employees who embezzle from them, and this is particularly true when the theft is of large amounts perpetrated by important officials (Bequai 1978, Krauss & MacGahan 1979, Lancaster & Hill 1981).

The common justification for failure to prosecute refers to "closing the barn door after the horse is gone"—the idea that prosecution will not return the stolen funds. However, we suspect that behind this rationalization two other motives operate. One is the shame—the poor "public relations"—of admitting that accounting controls were so lax that so much money could have been stolen without detection over-months or years. The other motive is that indicated by our hypothesis of "moral distance" (p. 14)—the hypothesis that people are judged less harshly when they commit the kinds of crimes we sense might be our possibility.

A Small Sample

In illustration, the Beverly Hills branch of the Wells Fargo Bank lost $21.3 million in about two years through a simple scheme (Lancaster & Hill 1981). The accused thief was the bank's operations officer in charge of bookkeeping functions. In accord with our maxim that "those who keep the books know how to cook the books" (Volume Three, Chapter 3), this official allegedly plundered the bank by moving computerized funds between "settlement accounts" in such an easy manner that he needed only 10 minutes every five days to siphon money into his pocket. He was caught only by chance when he filled out the wrong side of an "entry ticket" and sent it through the system.

The accused was able to get away with his crime, incidentally, because he was able to evade two of the checks against embezzlement recommended in the preceding volume. Financially sensitive duties were *not* rotated among officers, as prescribed, and this particular official either avoided taking his annual vacation or came back to the bank every fifth day to cover his depredations. However, the present point is that:

> the nation's 11th-largest bank tried for weeks to limit public disclosures concerning the embezzlement. But as auditors seeking to unravel the fraud slogged through thousands of daily inter-branch transactions involving millions of dollars, speculation mounted about the extent of the bank's problems. So [the Bank Chairman] decided to "go on the offensive." In part, he says, he wanted to scotch demoralizing rumors that fraud was pervasive among high-ranking officials at the bank's 383 branches. . . . Also, he says, he wanted to squelch reports that the bank was victimized by a big computer fraud. While knowledge of the safeguards built into the computer helped perpetuate the fraud, he concedes, "this was a systems fraud, not a computer fraud" (Lancaster & Hill 1981).

Resistance to "blowing the whistle" is common within large corporations and bureaucracies. Other examples abound.

When the president of Columbia Pictures Industries' movie and television units embezzled $61,000 from the company and forged an actor's name on a $10,000 check, he was given a leave of absence, a "clearance" by a psychiatrist who blamed the theft on "temporary emotional problems," and was then reinstated (not without opposition) as chief of movie and TV units (McClintick 1978).

Attempts to audit religious organizations that solicit funds for charities and "skim" some of the money are contested, and usually defeated, by the defense of "religious freedom" (*U.S. News & World Report* 1978).

The United States Department of Justice struggles with the Department of Labor to enforce laws against misuse and embezzlement of union pension funds (Frailey 1978).

Many corporate and governmental frauds constitute so-called "happy crimes" in which a circle of financial predators feeds off one another and passes the costs of their unproductive work to consumers. In this fashion large contractors, the entertainment industry, and big and small governments are prime candidates for bribes, kickbacks, and assorted larcenies concealed by "creative accounting" (Rowan 1980, Shaplen 1978).

In short, power makes it difficult to respond with justice to high-level financial cheats, but it can also distort justice in response to personal injuries and death. Thus Senator Edward M. Kennedy can have a motoring accident that results in the killing of his passenger under circumstances that would result in an ordinary citizen's indictment for negligent manslaughter. But he can plead guilty to the misdemeanor of leaving the scene of an accident and be given a two-month suspended jail sentence with revocation of his driver's license for one year (Barron 1980, Tedrow & Tedrow 1976). As the local prosecutor in that case put it:

> No matter how you cut it, you simply don't treat a United States Senator who is a criminal defendant the same way you treat a stockbroker. It's just one of the failings of human nature (Barron 1980, p. 186).

Justice yields to power. It is defended only by power that meets power.

SUMMARY

This brief excursion through the judicial process reminds us that doing justice is an ideal. This means that we aspire toward justice without ever producing it perfectly. Ideals are guides to action, but, by their very definition, they exceed what we achieve.

Response to crime is not only stimulated by a sense of justice; it is also proposed as an instrument with which to protect society by incapacitating and correcting offenders and by inhibiting others from yielding to criminal temptation. These topics concern the next chapters.

3 INCAPACITATING

Abstract • Societies attempt to protect themselves against crime by a moving mixture of responses. ∘ Arrest is a first step. ∘ Incapacitating offenders is a common secondary response. ∘ In addition, societies try to prevent crime, to correct offenders, and to deter criminal activity. • To incapacitate is to render an individual inoperative. ∘ Incapacitative procedures include execution, exile, mutilation, and incarceration. ∘ Western societies prefer incarceration as their principal mode of incapacitation. ∘ Measuring incarceration effects is made difficult by the possibility of side-effects. • Incarceration is justified, in part, by the L-shaped distribution of offenses graded by frequency and gravity. That is, many commit a few crimes, but a few commit many, and more serious, crimes. ∘ Acting on this justification carries the cost of false positives—jailing some offenders who are not dangerous. ∘ A sense of justice therefore modifies efficiency. • Mathematical models testing incarceration effects attempt to gauge the relation between the *actual* number of crimes that "kinds of criminals" will commit under present criminal justice conditions and the *possible* number of crimes such persons might commit if probability of conviction and/or duration of imprisonment were increased. ∘ Models express approximations, rather than certainties, because their major variables are estimated, rather than known. ∘ λ (lambda), the average number of crimes committed by a "kind of criminal" per year, is a crucial estimate. ∘ A table of assumed probabilities shows the sensitivity of mathematical models to changes in estimates of the probability of imprisonment, the length of incarceration, and lambda. • An Ohio project in test of incarceration effects on violent crimes concludes that a plausible and severe sentencing policy might reduce violent crime somewhere between seven and 27 percent per year, but at a high cost of false positives. • A California study comparing official records of career criminals with their unofficial confessions of criminality concludes that probabilities of arrest vary with the kinds of crime committed and range from zero to an implausible 100 percent. ∘ Authors of this study conclude that mandatory sentences can reduce crime but, again, at the cost of increasing prison populations. ∘ These researchers suggest that a "most efficient" policy of flat terms of 1.2 years for all felons would reduce serious crime by 20 percent per year and increase the prison population by 85 percent. This estimate is based on a particular, and small, number of career criminals. • An efficient policy would jail offenders at the peak of their careers, rather than toward the end. Such a policy runs into objections against incarcerating young felons. • Incarceration would be more efficient in reducing crime *if* likely repeaters could be identified early on. ∘ The more crime that is produced by fewer people, the greater the incapacitation effect. ∘ Failures in forecasting bad action reduce confidence in acting on this assumption. •

High crime zones presently have low probabilities of apprehending offenders and short periods of incarcerating them. Such areas are the ones that need incapacitation effects the most but, for such effects, they would pay the highest price in increased proportions of their populations in jails.

LIVING TOGETHER UNDER ONE CODE OF CONDUCT is always subject to challenge. It is particularly subject to challenge as diverse people of disparate talent and taste meet under the laws of one state.

Criminal activity constitutes one facet of challenge that persistently confronts social orders. Against this threat societies attempt to protect themselves in various ways. They do so by arresting miscreants, by incapacitating them, by trying to correct them or to prevent their development, and, most commonly, by adding sufficient costs to crimes as might deter offenders from repeating their depredations and others from yielding to similar temptations.

All these protective measures have been used "naturally," that is, impulsively, without attempts to rationalize them. They are most easily justified as commonsensical responses to crime when they are conceived as part of doing justice—as indicating reprobation and retribution. They are less easily justified when, as in modern societies, these protective measures are subjected to cost-benefit analyses and incapacitative tactics or reformative plans are tested for their effectiveness in achieving some end, such as a reduction in a crime rate.

A review of these tests confirms the thesis with which we began our discussion of response to crime—that what we *want to do* and what we are *willing to do* strongly affect efficiency. Simple efficiency does not determine policy, and no public policy in response to crime is perfectly rational.

Attempts to measure efficiency of allegedly protective tactics are made difficult by the fact that every procedure has side-effects. For example, it is difficult to assess the protective value of incapacitation because different modes of incapacitation may have different degrees of deterrent effect as well. Nevertheless, statisticians of social affairs have worked to provide estimates of the efficiency of several styles of incapacitation, reform, and deterrence, and we shall summarize their studies in this and succeeding chapters.

INCAPACITATION

To incapacitate is to render an individual inoperative. Many procedures can be used, and have been used, to reduce or eliminate offenders' abilities to perform crimes.

Execution is a sure incapacitative device. It has been historically popular and it is currently employed, but it is also presently deplored—deplored, at least, by some people for some offenders in some societies. However, the American Society of Criminology has taken an official stand, 1979, against execution *under any circumstances.*

Mutilation is another form of incapacitation practiced, for example, by Arabians in severing the hand(s) of repetitive thieves. It is also practiced by some Western states when they perform lobotomies to pacify recalcitrant violent offenders and surgical castrations[1] to control sex offenders (Bremer 1959).

Morality limits practicality, of course (p. 9). This point, a simple one it seems, is nevertheless difficult for many students to understand because they think that what they regard as moral is necessarily rational. The difference is illustrated, in the present context, by a Pittsburgh judge's dilemma:

United Press International (1980d): CASTRATION REJECTED FOR CONVICTED RAPIST
A county judge says castrating a convicted killer and rapist would be an "obvious remedy," but he said he does not favor it.

Allegheny County Common Pleas Judge John W. O'Brien said he opposed the measure for religious and ethical reasons after sentencing Russell Williams to a maximum 15–30 years in prison Tuesday for his conviction of rape and terroristic threats.

O'Brien said Wednesday that society is helpless to deal with criminals like Williams—"What do you do with a man like that? Send him back to prison to rape another fellow inmate?"

Williams, 32, formerly of Philadelphia, was convicted of raping a fellow inmate at Western Penitentiary.

He is also serving a term for murder, the rape of a female, and is accused of two other rapes.

The judge said Wednesday that castration "would be an obvious remedy," but he did not favor castrating convicted rapists because "dismembering anyone goes against my sense of religion and ethics."

"I am afraid he will go back to the prison and continue to rape young inmates," the judge said. "Society is practically unable to deal with a situation like that."

Exile is yet another mode of incapacitating offenders, but it is a procedure that now offends Western sensibilities but not Communist

[1] Hormonal castration is more effective than surgical castration in controlling some aggressive sex offenders (Money 1970). However, chemical castration requires continued administration of an androgen-depleting hormone.

ethics (Chalidze 1977, Connor 1972, Hollander 1973). Nevertheless, the idea of banishing[2] offenders is revived from time to time. A former solicitor general of Alberta has recommended self-sufficient arctic settlements for persistent bad actors. An American lawyer (Kutner 1968) has suggested putting recalcitrant criminals in orbit in a space colony. He reasons that prisons will overflow by the year 2000 and that a population of 7 to 10 million convicts can best be contained in an escape-free spacecraft.

Today incarceration substitutes for exile in most industrialized countries and, while jailing people is an ancient practice, it is only in the last 200 years that it has become a popular response to crime in European and North American cultures. The costs of incarcerating criminals are incalculable and the rationality of this response cannot therefore be precisely assessed.

Incarceration Effects

On any day in Western countries, between 80 and 200 persons are in jails and prisons for every 100,000 people in the population. They are kept caged at an annual cost per inmate that ranges between 12 and 30 thousand 1980-US-dollars and their equivalents.

These estimates are crude because, even in those industrialized countries that diligently measure themselves, tallies are confusing. Sometimes they separate and sometimes they mix juvenile and adult offenders, those in federal, provincial (state), county, and municipal cells, and those incarcerated full-time and part-time. Tallies also sometimes include, and sometimes exclude, persons in military prisons, in relatively "open" settings like work camps, and those in half-way houses. Furthermore, estimates are frequently translated into crude rates per 100,000 population rather than refined rates based on the sex and age composition that is at risk. In some cases, the census base is eight or nine years out of date.

Figures on the costs of incarceration are similarly crude and vary with what is counted. These costs obviously include more than the construction of prisons and the maintenance of buildings, guards,

---

[2] Exile is sometimes distinguished from banishment. Exile refers to removal of the offender from his/her place of residence with enforced settlement, permanently or for a term, in a fixed abode. Banishment excludes the offender from his/her familiar neighborhood and, perhaps, from particular kinds of places, such as urban centers, without otherwise fixing his/her domicile.

Both exile and banishment are expressions of the classic *anthropoemic* response—throwing the person out.

and inmates. They also include the burden of maintaining prisoners' dependents and the inestimable costs of prison riot, rape, murder, and moral infection. Nevertheless, Robison (1969) calculates a "ballpark" estimate that legal response to American *robbers* costs as much, or more, than what the robbers steal. Catching and imprisoning *burglars* may cost one-and-a-half to three times the value of their loot.

Even with such rough estimates, it appears that incarceration is more expensive than exile or execution, but it is deemed more humane by contemporary civilizations. This judgment represents a modern morality, not one that has been historically approved.

Defenders of the practice of imprisonment point to its incapacitative efficiency. They claim that, for as long as the convict is caged, s(he) is prevented from committing crimes against the citizenry at large, but not, of course, against the convict's peers and guardians. Efficiency is simply assumed and rarely assessed against any standards of costs and benefits. That is, we do not know *how much it is worth*—in terms of crime reduction—to keep this or that kind of offender locked up, given the costs of his/her keep.

Whatever these costs may sum to in the average citizen's reckoning, they may seem a reasonable price to pay for isolating "mad-dog" killers, but they seem a high price for restraining run-of-the-mill burglars and robbers who annually steal much less than the cost of their incarceration. But, of course, satisfaction of justice is not included in this assessment, and justice is worth something, although it is seldom priced.

ESTIMATES OF INCARCERATION EFFECTS

Criminologists have attempted to calculate the costs and benefits of physically restraining offenders. They have attempted to measure incarceration effects separate from deterrent and reformative effects. Imprisonment may have such ancillary effects, but what one wishes to assess in testing the incarceration hypothesis[3] is how many crimes are prevented by keeping bad actors locked up.

The plausibility of this hypothesis is encouraged by a host of studies showing that a few serious offenders commit a large proportion of the "heavy" crimes. This fact is verified by asking people about the

[3] Reseachers commonly refer to this hypothesis as that of "incapacitation." However, in actuality they are not testing the effects of all modes of incapacitation but, rather, the effect of the particular tactic of imprisonment.

For convenience we shall use the terms "incapacitation" and "incarceration" interchangeably, with recognition that jailing is only one form of incapacitation.

frequency and gravity of their crimes as well as by official records of depredations. The typical curve of confessed and observed criminality, weighted by frequency and seriousness of offenses, is an L-curve, or J-curve if plotted in the other direction (Elmhorn 1965). This means that many people commit a few minor offenses, but only a few people commit serious offenses repetitively. This is the same kind of distribution, incidentally, that we find when we count degrees of observance of most moral conduct (Allport 1934, 1939, Farnsworth 1949, pp. 543–544, Harvey 1935).

A similar finding derives from following a cohort of youngsters and counting their "police contacts." When Wolfgang and his associates (1972) did this with all males born in 1945 who lived in Philadelphia from their 10th through 17th years, they counted 3,475 boys (35%) of a total 9,945 who had recorded police contacts. But 627 of these delinquents had five or more such experiences with the police and were therefore designated "chronic offenders." These chronic offenders, constituting 18 percent of the delinquents, committed more than half of the known crimes and were responsible, in particular, for the more serious crimes. In addition, the more a boy repeated offenses, the more serious his crimes became. Youthful careers may not specialize in one kind of crime, but as they lengthen they graduate in gravity.

The fact of the L-curve distribution of crimes by frequency and gravity among a population—the fact that a few account for much—has made it seem plausible that caging this minority of bad actors would economically reduce crime. This is the reasoning that justifies recommendations for mandatory sentences, although such required restraint is also justified by appeals to deterrence and justice.

For example, Wolfgang and Collins (1977) reckon from their longitudinal study of Philadelphia youth that each year of imprisonment of each chronic offender would prevent 2.4 felonies, although many of these crimes would not have been known to the police. They also estimate that jailing all male felons from their 14th through 17th years would prevent the commission of an additional four or five "index crimes"[4] per year. When Wolfgang and Collins weigh the possible impact of incarcerating male felons between the ages of 15 and 30, they estimate that for the one year, 1974, imprisoning these men

[4] The FBI's annual Uniform Crime Reports catalog seven "index crimes" analyzed as the violent crimes of murder, forcible rape, aggravated assault, and robbery, and the property crimes of burglary, larceny-theft, and automobile theft.

would have prevented 1,171 known index crimes and reduced the Philadelphia crime rate for that year by two percent.

Two difficulties intrude: One concerns estimates of the real amount of crime each offender would produce per year if s(he) were *not* jailed. The other difficulty concerns the size of a prison population required to reduce crime by a certain proportion, given that new generations of crime-possible youth are added to the free population each year.

Justice and Utility Again

Actuaries have attempted to estimate incarceration effects and have begun their work by distinguishing two kinds of incapacitative policy. Greenberg (1975) calls restraint "selective incapacitation" if it is imposed on convicts who are predicted to recidivate if released before x-years. Such predictive or preventive confinement is employed, but it is criticized as unjust because it keeps people in prison not so much for the crimes they have committed as for the crimes prophesied to be committed if the offender is released "too soon."

On the other hand, Greenberg calls restraint "collective incapacitation" if it reduces crime by sentencing offenders for what they have done *without* attempting to select those who are more or less likely to be repeaters. Obviously, if we could predict criminality more accurately than we do at present, then selective incapacitation would have greater crime-reducing effects than collective incapacitation. However, given the poor state of the art of forecasting dangerous acts (Chapter 4), many criminologists regard selective incarceration as less fair than collective incapacitation (Cohen 1978, p. 189). As a result of this sense of justice, tests of incarceration effects have been tests of collective incapacitation.

Models

Mathematical models of incarceration effects attempt to relate an estimate of the *actual* criminality of a class of offenders, given some state of a criminal justice system, to the *possible* number of crimes that might be prevented by changing the probability and duration of incapacitation.

The relationship between actual criminality and potential criminality is calculated by assuming a probability of being convicted for each crime of a particular type before an offender commits his or her next crime, multiplied by the probability of being imprisoned if one is convicted, multiplied by the average length of prison term for such crime, with this result multiplied, in turn, by the number of crimes committed annually by the average criminal of that category. Reuel and Shlomo Shinnar (1975, p. 588) suggest a formula for estimating the number of crimes prevented by incarceration as follows:

$$\text{Effective reduction} = 1 - \frac{1}{1 + \lambda q J S}$$

where:

q = probability of conviction per crime committed,
J = probability of imprisonment if convicted,
S = average length of a prison term served for that kind of crime, and
λ (lambda) = the crime rate per year per criminal of that "type."

All mathematical models rest on assumptions, of course, and also on the ability to assign valid tallies to the variables that they include as causal. Thus this model assumes what is probably false—that there is no deterrent effect. The Shinnars note that, "We assume the number of criminals is unaffected by the crime policy" (p. 587). However, no one knows the size of an active, sporadic, or potential "criminal population" or the thresholds of temptation that increase or decrease that population.

Furthermore, this construction of the working of a criminal justice system also assumes that imprisonment is not criminogenic. That is, it discounts the possibility that jailing people makes them more criminal upon their release than they would otherwise have been.

In addition, this model assumes that the average probability of a criminal's being convicted of a given crime (q):

> . . . is equal to the fraction of crimes solved by conviction. . . . In other words, we attribute the majority of unsolved crimes to criminals who are convicted at least once. . . . This is crucial. 70% of all safety crimes in the United States are never solved and in New York City this fraction is higher. If most crimes are committed by criminals who are never caught, then no incapacitative policy will work until there are means to catch them at least once (Shinnar & Shinnar 1975, p. 592).

Yet another trouble with mathematical models of a criminal justice system is that of assigning correct numbers to the variables it includes. Some jurisdictions, but not all, provide data that permit assignment of approximate numbers to q (the probability of conviction),[5] J (the probability of imprisonment), and S (average

---

[5] The Shinnars show that qJS is equal to $q_a J_a S$, where the subscript, a, refers to arrest. "Both $q_a J_a$ and qJ are just the overall probability that a crime will result in a commitment" (p. 589, n.12).

sentence served). Thus the Shinnars show that in New York State the probability of a convict spending time in jail declined between 1960 and 1970. They estimate that the chances of being sent to prison if one committed a crime (qJ) declined as follows (Table 3.1):

Table 3.1 Probability of Being Imprisoned (qJ) in New York State for Classes of Crime, 1960 and 1970*

	1960	1970
Violent Crimes**	.09	.027
Safety Crimes†	.034	.008
All Felonies	.03	.0058

*Abstracted, with permission, from S. & R. Shinnar, "The effects of the criminal justice system on the control of crime: A quantitative approach." *Law & Society Review,* 1975, 9:581–611 (Table 2). © 1975 by The Law and Society Association.
**Violent Crimes include murder, rape, robbery, and assault.
†Safety crimes are violent crimes plus burglary. Burglary is added because a forced entry can lead to robbery or homicide if the burglar is apprehended in the act.

These investigators also calculate that the average time spent in prison per crime in New York changed as per Table 3.2.

Table 3.2 Average Time Spent in Prison Per Conviction (qJS) by Class of Crime, New York State, 1960 and 1970*

	1960	1970
Violent Crimes	.35	.06
Safety Crimes	.13	.029
All Felonies	.1	.0175

*Reprinted, with permission, from Shinnar and Shinnar, *op. cit.,* Table 2.

A more important difficulty of these models lies in estimating λ (lambda), the average number of crimes committed per criminal per year. This number is an unknown, yet this estimate is crucial because incarceration effects will differ greatly with the distribution of offenses among offenders. For example, if 100 miscreants commit 100 crimes per year—one apiece—then locking up one convict for one year prevents only one crime. On the other hand, if 10 offenders commit those 100 crimes, then jailing one convict for one year prevents 10 crimes.

As we shall see, there are a few informed estimates of lambda, but an appreciation of the sensitivity of the Shinnars's formula to changes in lambda is given by a table of probabilities presented by Wilson and Boland (1976). Table 3.3 shows how the Shinnars's model applies for two assumed values of lambda, two and 10, and for seven probabilities of imprisonment, ranging from .03 to .09, and for four average prison terms, ranging from two years to four.

Table 3.3 Percentage Reduction in Expected Crime Rate Due to Increases in Probability of Imprisonment and Average Time Served From Current Values (i.e., .03, 2) for Two Values of Lambda

Average Number of Years Served	Lambda = 2				Lambda = 10			
	2.0	2.5	3.0	4.0	2.0	2.5	3.0	4.0
Probability of Imprisonment								
.03	—	2.6	5.1	9.7	—	8.6	15.8	27.2
.04	3.4	6.7	9.7	15.2	11.1	20.0	27.3	38.5
.05	6.7	10.4	13.8	20.0	20.0	28.9	36.0	46.7
.06	9.7	13.8	17.6	24.3	27.3	36.0	42.9	53.0
.07	12.5	17.0	21.1	28.2	33.3	41.8	48.3	58.9
.08	15.2	20.0	24.3	31.7	38.5	46.7	53.0	62.0
.09	17.6	22.8	27.3	34.9	42.9	50.8	56.8	65.2

(Probability of imprisonment and average time served based on 1970 state prison population figures, 1970 adult Index Crimes [estimated], and assume 21 percent of jail population is serving a one-year sentence for an Index Crime).

*Reproduced with permission from J.Q. Wilson and B. Boland, "Crime." In W. Gorham and N. Glazer (eds.), *The Urban Predicament.* © 1976 by The Urban Institute.

This table allows estimates of the *marginal* reduction in crime—that is, the reduction beyond present rates produced by present practices—if either the probability of imprisonment or the time served, or both, were increased. The low probability of incarceration for index crimes—three chances in a hundred—and the estimated average sentence length—two years—are based on 1970 American data. Table 3.3 can be read, then, to yield such estimates as the following:

1. that doubling the probability of going to prison for the present average stay of two years from 3/100 to 6/100 would reduce index crimes by 9.7 percent.

2. that increasing time served from the present average of two years to three years, with the probability of imprisonment remaining constant, would reduce index crimes by 5.1 percent.

3. that simultaneously doubling the probability of imprisonment and lengthening time served to three years would reduce serious crime by 17.6 percent or, if lambda were actually 10, by 42.9 percent.

These conditional statements should not be taken literally; they are hypotheticals based on assumptions of average criminal activity and probabilities of arrest, conviction, and incarceration. Lambda, in particular, is an unknown, but two tallies—one in Ohio and one in California—give us an appreication of the likely trade-off between incarceration and crime.

The Dangerous Offender Project

Van Dine, Conrad, and Dinitz (1979) obtained the criminal records of 342 suspects arrested for violent crimes in Franklin County (Columbus), Ohio, during 1973. The crimes charged included homicide, forcible rape, aggravated assault, and robbery. Only 166 (46.5%) of these men were *convicted* of the crimes charged but, to give the incapacitation argument its best test, the investigators assumed that all those arrested were guilty and furthermore that, if they were charged with several crimes but only convicted of one or two, the total number of charged offenses would be tallied as providing a more realistic picture of offenders' criminal activities.

With these assumptions, Van Dine and his colleagues analyzed individual histories to ascertain how much violent crime would have been prevented if these miscreants had been in prison in 1973. They discovered that more than half of these defendants had no previous felony conviction, either as adults or as juveniles. More than two-thirds were first-time adult felony convicts. This immediately reduces the possibility that their 1973 violence could have been prevented by earlier incarceration. However, 12 percent of these men had two prior felony convictions and 18 percent had three or more such convictions.

The researchers then applied 18 hypothetical sentencing practices to assess how much of the 1973 violence could have been avoided by differential incarceration at these offenders' last previous convictions. For example, one sentencing option tested was that, for any first violent conviction, a five-year fixed term would have been imposed—that is, a term with no parole and no time off for good behavior. This sentencing policy also assumed that, for their non-violent crimes, these offenders would have been sentenced as per current law in Ohio. However, the most severe sentencing practice tested assumed that, with *any* indictable conviction, violent or non-violent, these men would have received a five-year fixed term. In other words, it was assumed that, even for a first offense, a convicted auto thief or grand larcenist would have been locked up for five years.

With the most severe, plausible sentencing policy in effect, and assuming that those accused in 1973 were guilty, regardless of their conviction or acquittal, 111 violent attacks (3.8%) of the 2,892 recorded violent crimes would have been prevented in that year. If only those *convicted* in 1973 had been so incarcerated, the savings is reduced to 1.7 percent of such crimes.

These are tallies of possible violent crime reduction for *one year.* The total number of crimes that would have been forestalled by jailing these men for five years on conviction of their first felony depends on assumptions about the annual rate—lambda—at which these men would have committed felonies had they not been jailed. In addition, these estimates are lowered by exclusion of juvenile records. During the reference year, for the United States as a whole, one-fourth of all persons arrested for violent crimes were juveniles. Incarceration of these men upon their first juvenile felony would increase the estimate of crime prevention.

With these qualifications, Van Dine and his associates conclude that:

> **1.** Application of our most severe sentencing policy, which provides for a flat five-year term for any adult or juvenile convicted of a felony, would have prevented the 210 violent crimes for which arrests were made in 1973, or 7.3 percent of the 2,892 such crimes reported. But the number of crimes for which a conviction was obtained constituted 3.6 percent of the total.
>
> **2.** Assuming that recidivists commit the same proportion of uncleared crimes as they commit of those cleared by the police, it is possible that 26.7 percent of the reported crimes of violence might have been prevented.
>
> **3.** If it is assumed that recidivists committed a larger percentage of the uncleared crimes than they did of the cleared crimes, the number of crimes prevented would exceed 26.7 percent.
>
> **4.** The most reasonable and probable effect of [the severe] sentencing policy is a prevention level falling between 7.3 and 26.7 percent. Our opinion is that this level must be less than the upper limit because recidivists are more liable to arrest . . . than are virgins in crime.

5. A more reasonable sentencing policy, five years incarceration on a second felony conviction, to be imposed on both juveniles and adults, will yield prevention values of 4.7 percent at the level of arrest . . . and 2.1 percent at the conviction level. If these values are extrapolated to account for the uncleared crimes, the prevention value will rise to about 17 percent.

6. If incapacitating sentences are reserved for violent offenders only . . . five years for any violent felony, whether committed by adult or juvenile offenders, the number of violent offenses prevented in 1973 would constitute 2.7 percent at the level of arrest, and 1.7 percent at the level of conviction. The extrapolation for uncleared offenses would yield a prevention value of 9.8 percent.

7. There is substantial variability in the preventive potential by category of offense. [With the severe policy—five years flat for any felony] whereby 26.7 percent of the reported cleared felonies would have been prevented, we find that 34.4 percent of the murders, 29.9 percent of the robberies, 25.5 percent of the forcible sex offenses, and only 12.9 percent of the aggravated assaults would have been prevented.

8. To accomplish the goals of [this sentencing policy] would result in the increase of commitments from Franklin County by about 500–600 percent.

9. We collected data to establish the percentage of those who would have been confined under a policy of sentencing violent offenders to five years in prison but who in fact did not commit a subsequent violent crime. Of the universe of 164 adults arrested for a crime of violence in 1966, 93 were convicted, 88 were returned to the community, and nine were reconvicted within five years of street time of a violent crime. This yields a percentage of false-positives amounting to 90 percent, an intolerable margin of error (reprinted by permission of the publisher from *Restraining the Wicked* by Stephan Van Dine, John P. Conrad, and Simon Dinitz, pages 115–116. Lexington Books, D.C. Heath & Company. Copyright 1979, D.C. Heath and Company).

Summary

Incarceration reduces the amount of violent crime by a small proportion at a cost of increasing the size of the prison population and containing many men who do not repeat their violence. This statement of *incarceration* effects is exclusive of any possible *deterrent* effects on others that incapacitating convicts may have. The low gain and high cost of present, or plausible, incarceration is explained by three facts:

1. Violent juveniles are not part of the tally. The most active period in men's violent careers is between the ages of 16 and 22. *If*

crime reduction were the sole objective of a criminal justice system—
and it is not—then identifying and confining young men at the peak
of their criminal careers would be more effective than confining
older, multiple offenders toward the end of their violent times. But
such a policy would require a drastic change in attitude toward
youths and their crimes.

2. The pool of official recidivists is small, and lambda is not known.

3. Even among recidivists, their *known rate* of repetition is too
low. to produce much reduction in crime through their
incapacitation.

This statement assumes, again, that uncleared offenses are *not* the
doings of this minority of apprehended criminals.

California Criminal Careers

Petersilia, Greenwood, and Lavin (1978) provide another test of
possible incarceration effects with data from the 49 career criminals
they studied in California. These investigators estimate probability of
arrest by relating prisoners' *official records* to their *confessions* of
criminal activity. They find probabilities that range from a low of zero
for a drug sales to an implausible high of 1.00 (certainty) for rape, as
indicated in Table 3.4.

Table 3.4 Career Criminals' Probability of Arrest*

Offense	Self-Reported Number of Crimes Committed	Number of Arrests on Record	Probability of Arrest[a]
Auto theft	594	27	.04
Theft over $50 + purse snatching	560	20	.04
Burglary	873	76	.09
Robbery	844	110	.13
Aggravated assault	85	26	.31
Forgery/NSF	632	49	.08
Drug sales	2,358	0	0
Rape	3	4	1.00

[a]Probability of arrest = proportion of self-reported crimes that resulted in
a recorded arrest (except for the anomalous rape data).

*Reproduced from J. Petersilia, P.W. Greenwood, and M. Lavin, *Criminal
Careers of Habitual Felons.* Table 18. 1978. Washington, D.C.: U.S. Department of Justice.

Table 3.4 shows that there is a loose connection between a career criminal's offense rate and his arrest rate. Property crimes in particular were low-risk crimes for these men during the 20 years, on the average, that they engaged in an assortment of depredations.

In a separate assessment, Petersilia and Greenwood (1977) estimate how much crime might be reduced by keeping offenders incarcerated. It should be noted, again, that their estimate of incapacitation effects says nothing about crime reduction through deterrence, that is, it does not address the question of how much crime is reduced by threat of punishment made realistic through imprisonment of a particular proportion of convicts. With this proviso, Petersilia and Greenwood conclude that:

> Mandatory sentences can reduce crime as a result of incapacitation effects but the increase in prison population may be unacceptably large. To reduce crime by half, every convicted offender would have to be imprisoned for five years. If only defendants who have a prior adult conviction are imprisoned, the crime-reduction effect is about half the effect produced by sentencing every convicted felon to prison. This analysis suggests that the most efficient policy is to sentence all convicted felons to 1.2 years of prison, resulting in a 20 percent reduction in the crime rate, and raising the prison population by 85 percent.

SUMMARY

1. Estimates of incarceration effects do *not* include possible ancillary deterrent and reformative effects.

2. It is reasonable to assume that young bad actors are likely to repeat crimes if they are not restrained. This is particularly true of the low pay-off, but high-annoyance, crimes of burglary, robbery, and vandalism.

Restraint takes many forms, of which incarceration is only one. But, however restraint is imposed, it directly reduces crime in the free population for the time the offender is held.

3. Estimates of incarceration effects are only approximations because we do not know individual *rates* of criminal activity or *length* of career for *categories* of offender.

4. If individuals have *varying* crime rates, assuming lambda as the *average* of all criminals' activities *under*estimates actual incapacitation effects.

5. The *more* crime that is produced by *fewer* people—that is, the greater the proportion of repeaters in a population—the *larger* the expected reduction in crime for incapacitation.

6. The *higher* the probability of incapacitation per crime committed and the *longer* the period of incapacitation, the *greater* the expected reduction in crime.

7. Jurisdictions with *low probabilities* of incarcerating offenders and with *short periods* of incarceration require the *greatest expansion* of their prison populations in order to produce a given reduction in crime.

American data suggest that zones of high crime presently have low probabilities of incarceration and short sentences. For example, Cohen (1978, p. 255) reports that:

> For the 29 states in 1970 for which data are available, the correlation between the index crime rate and the probability of imprisonment per crime is −.64. . . . The correlation between the index crime rate and the expected time served per crime (given by the product of the probability of imprisonment per crime and the average time served by those imprisoned) is −.55. For violent crimes in the same 29 states these correlations are −.54 and −.64, respectively.

This means that the areas that need the incapacitation effect most will pay the highest price for it. This also means that criminologists are motivated, but hard put, to invent more efficient and morally palatable substitutes for present prisons (Chapter 7).

If it is difficult to measure incapacitative effects and to derive public policy from such measurement, it is equally difficult to predict dangerous behavior and to measure deterrent effects, as the next chapters show.

4 PREDICTING DANGER

Abstract • Citizens and their courts ask experts to predict dangerous conduct. • Distinctions are drawn between three modes of anticipating the future: prophecy, forecast, and prediction. • Four difficulties beset attempts to predict dangerous behavior. ○ One difficulty lies in the vagueness of the idea of "dangerousness." Different definitions, and different criteria by which to identify the defined acts, produce varied tallies of dangerous people. ○ Another difficulty resides in the fact that all forecasts demand that a price be paid for correct prediction in the currency of error. 1. The relative *probabilities* of accurate and inaccurate forecasts are one consideration. 2. The *value* of these estimates is another consideration that varies with the events being predicted and with the interests of concerned assessors. ○ A third difficulty concerns the different populations within which dangerous individuals are to be detected. "Refining" the population at risk increases predictive power. ○ A fourth difficulty occurs because probabilities of action depend on contingencies, and contingencies are not easy to foresee. • Epidemiological research confirms the advice to count on continuity. • A tragic story illustrates the imperfect state of the art of predicting danger and the risks of discounting continuity. • It is easier to construct private policy than public policy from imperfect estimates of future events. ○ This occurs because individual actors more frequently experience the consequences of their acts than do societal engineers. ○ However, the loving connection urges individuals to accept a higher probability of attack from loved ones than from strangers. ○ The notion of "disposition" is relevant to the prediction of danger. • It is concluded that: ○ Accuracy of forecast is improved by *narrowing* the population base of persons at risk of being violent. ○ The importance assigned to predictions is a function of the *probabilities* assigned to positive and negative bets, the *values* placed on each of these probabilities, and the *range* of probability exhibited by the events of interest. ○ There *are* carriers of violence who are to be recognized by counting continuities in conduct.

WE COMMONLY INCARCERATE INDIVIDUALS in prisons and hospitals in order to protect peaceful people from violent ones. In the case of violent actors who have been convicted of crimes, this justification is sometimes confounded with the urge to do justice by punishing offenders. Nevertheless, the socially protective function of confining bad actors seeks confirmation from behavioral science that those who are dangerous are locked up while less menacing offenders are released after serving a fair sentence. These desires place the burden of foresight[1] upon selected experts.

In Western societies, psychiatrists and psychologists are asked by citizens and their courts to predict "dangerousness." It is hoped that a specialized course of study will have produced tools, and experts to use them, who can then make informed decisions, rather than guesses, about the likely careers of a variety of violent persons.

There is some such expertise, but it provides cold comfort to those who expect a foolproof answer to the predictive question, "Will he do it again?" The usual answer does not satisfy the "utility" sought by most inquirers. Furthermore, the best answer we have been able to devise thus far rests heavily on foretelling the future of a career from its past, allowing for sex differences in the behavior being anticipated and for changes in behavior with age. This is to say that our best answer to the predictive question assumes the theme of "contingent continuity," as described in Volume One, Chapter 3.

Answers to predictive questions are made difficult for four related reasons: The acts to be predicted are often vaguely defined, all forecasts carry costs, the populations within which predictions are made vary, and human action is not uniformly caused.

VAGUE DANGERS

If the predictive question is asked solely about "dangerousness," the answer is uncertain because that term covers much behavioral

---

[1] Modes of foretelling the future have been described in Volume One, Chapter 3. It was argued there that it is useful to distinguish three techniques: Prophecy, forecast, and prediction.

Briefly, a *prophecy* is a statement about the likely course of events made either from private cues or from public cues that have little or no empirical warrant. "Reading" a crystal ball is an example of prophecy from private signs; astrology is an example of prophecy from public signs that have little empirical backing.

A *forecast* is a statement about the likely course of events made from public cues for which there is empirical warrant. However, these cues may or may not be causes of the events being foretold and, in either case, the forecaster has no control over those signs. Foretelling the weather is an example of forecasting.

A *prediction,* by contrast, is like a forecast in its public nature and empirically warranted cues, but it is made in cases in which the predictor can manipulate the probable causes of the events being foretold. A prediction says, on the basis of public evidence, that, "If you do this, then so many times in a hundred, you will get that."

For literary convenience, the terms "forecast" and "prediction" will be used interchangeably, but it should be recognized that, technically, they refer to different powers.

ground. The concept specifies no particular act, and it probably cannot. The idea is used to refer to an assortment of behaviors including child abuse, spouse battering, drunkenness, sexual assault, robbery, wounding, homicide, and, at times, an assortment of property offenses.

Some investigators have extended the notion of "dangerous" to those who have committed *any crime* or to those who have invoked the insanity defense (Goldstein & Katz 1960). Other scholars would include having "violent thoughts" as a criterion of "dangerousness" (Ervin & Lion 1969) and, in a court case, it was decided that the habitual writing of bad checks was a mark of "dangerousness" (*U.S.* v. *Charnizon* 1967).

Maryland's law (1951), now abrogated, that allowed indeterminate sentencing of the "defective delinquent" defined such a person:

> ... as an individual who, by the demonstration of persistent aggravated anti-social or criminal behavior, evidences a propensity toward criminal activity, and who is found to have either such intellectual deficiency or emotional unbalance, or both, as to clearly demonstrate an actual *danger* to society (Defective Delinquent Statute, Article 31B, emphasis added).

In assessing the correctional programs based on this law, and located at the Patuxent Institution, Gordon (1977, p. 240) reasons that "danger" should include a history of attacks on property as well as on persons since such attacks threaten the social fabric.

In summary, then, when experts are asked to foresee "dangerousness," they may be asked a mixture of questions such as these:

1. How *serious* will the attack of the "dangerous" person be?
2. What is the expected *nature* of that attack?
3. Under what *circumstance* is the attack likely?
4. How *probable* is such an attack under that circumstance?
5. How *frequently* will such violence occur?
6. How *imminent* is the danger?

For example, in *Cross* v. *Harris,* Judge David Bazelon (1969) defined "dangerous persons" as those "likely to attack or otherwise inflict injury, loss, pain, or other evil" and asked for judgment of the probable recurrence of the instant crime, the probable frequency of such acts, and the magnitude of the harm likely to be done.

None of these estimates is specific. No *degree* of probability is indicated nor is the *kind* of probability identified (see pp. 82–83). And, of course, the evidence on which such forecast is to be made is left open.

Researchers on this topic have attempted to refine questions asked about "dangerousness" by specifying the kinds of criminal violence to be predicted. They prefer, then, to speak of "dangerous behaviors" rather than of "dangerousness." In this vein, Cocozza and Steadman (1974) devised a "Legal Dangerousness Scale" to be used in identifying persons likely to commit robbery, aggravated assault, forcible rape, or homicide. In keeping with the premises of "contingent continuity," this measure is a tally of an individual's career in crime, scored from 0 to 15.[2]

In resolution of the identification problem, Monahan (1978) suggests that future research use "multiple definitions of violence":

> Violence should be defined in a hierarchy including (a) the four FBI violent index crimes of murder, forcible rape, robbery, and aggravated assault, and (b) all assaultive acts against persons (p. 251).

Monahan reasons that broader definitions increase accuracy of foresight. He notes:

> Large targets are easier to hit than small ones. The data bear out this axiom. One attempt to predict "assaultive behavior" had 16 percent true positives when the criterion was defined as "homicide, all assaults, attempted murder, battery, forcible rape and attempt to rape"; 22.6 percent true positives when the criterion was expanded to include "other sex offenses and kidnapping"; and 53 percent true positives when assaultive behavior was construed still more loosely to encompass "all of the above plus robbery, all sex offenses, weapon offenses and disturbing the peace" (cited in Halatyn 1975). (p. 252).

The Criterion Problem

The scope of the definition of "dangerousness" is one problem; the criteria by which behaviors denoted by a definition are to be identified is another problem.

The usual criteria of arrest or conviction are important, but they grossly *under*estimate violence. Surveys of citizens inquiring about their victimization indicate that only 40 to 50 percent of FBI-defined "violent crime" is reported to the police. Perhaps 60 to 70 percent of "simple assaults" go unreported (U.S. Department of Justice 1974), and such attacks are undoubtedly differently defined by different segments of any large population.

---

[2] The Legal Dangerousness Scale awards 8 points for any "severe" juvenile record, 4 points to a person who has been jailed two or more times prior to the present incarceration, 2 points for a history of violent crime, and 1 point if the instant offense is more serious than such "morals" charges as gambling or selling or using drugs.

In addition, police frequently take bad actors to mental hospitals rather than arrest them. Much of such referral for violent behavior could as well have resulted in arrest. For example, Cocozza and Steadman (1974, p. 1013) note that some patients released from a mental hospital for the criminally insane were returned to hospital "for behavior very similar to that displayed by other patients who were arrested for violent crimes."

In corroboration of this finding, Jacobson and colleagues (1973) report that one-third of police referrals to a forensic clinic in Los Angeles was occasioned by "aggressive behavior" that did not result in arrest.

Given these shortfalls in reporting a range of violent acts to the police, Monahan (1978, p. 256) recommends that self-reports be used as an additional criterion against which to test the accuracy of forecasters and their tools. In particular, he suggests employment of Toch's (1969) method of "peer interview," in which parolees are trained as research assistants to interview other parolees about their violent behavior.

Identification

If, then, we resolve some of the difficulty of defining "danger" by specifying a family of crimes that we have in mind, and if we employ combined criteria such as arrest, hospitalization, and self-report measures, we *can* identify pools of bad actors. But all such identification exacts a price in its application.

COST OF FORECAST

A review of Volume One, Chapter 3, tells us that valid tests of particular kinds of behavior may not be accurate predictors of that behavior. This is especially the case when the acts to be forecast are rare events or popular ones. In such cases, most tests (combinations of cues) do *not* improve foresight over that which is given from information about the frequency (base rate) with which such behavior is exhibited in a particular population.

When we attempt to gauge the probability that individuals will commit an infrequent crime like homicide, we pay a price in the form of a large number of *false positive predictions*. That is, along with our correct identification of violent people, we incorrectly identify as violent numbers of people who turn out to be relatively peaceful. This is particularly the case when the population base is heterogeneous with respect to the kinds of events being anticipated and the behavior to be foretold is either extremely rare or common. In a *general* population, every test thus far devised to identify probably dangerous persons does so by incorrectly specifying many individuals who do not become as dangerous as predicted in the fashion predicted. This does not mean that such tests may not single out more and less dangerous people, since there are degrees and qualities of violent action and situational contingencies that affect outcomes. But it does mean that many people who give violent signs do not behave as violently as we expect when we rely on those cues.

Livermore et al. (1968) provide a clear statement of the price to be paid in false positives for a certain quantity of true predictions:

> Assume that one person out of a thousand will kill. Assume also that an exceptionally accurate test is created which differentiates with ninety-five percent effectiveness those who will kill from those who will not. If 100,000 people were tested, out of the 100 who would kill, 95 would be isolated. Unfortunately, out of the 99,900 who would not kill, 4,995 people would also be isolated as potential killers. In these circumstances, it is clear that we could not justify incarcerating all 5,090 people. If, in the criminal law, it is better that ten guilty men go free than that one innocent man suffer, how can we say in the civil commitment area that it is better that fifty-four harmless people be incarcerated lest one dangerous man be free? (p. 84).

Livermore's example refers to attempts to foretell rare events in a heterogeneous population. However, pages 87–90 will indicate that we can reduce predictive error by narrowing the population base, that is, by isolating subsets of the general population with higher frequencies of the behavior in which we are interested. This is what is meant by "refining" the rate.

Nevertheless, every diagnosis from which a prediction is made confronts the policy question of what price is to be paid, and by whom, for correct predictions in the currency of false predictions. This cost of decision applies whether the judgments on which we are betting are medical, marital, educational, vocational, psychiatric, or criminological.

The cues which we have combined into some test with which to forecast violent behavior always carry costs. The costs are differently priced depending on the purposes of the forecaster and on the values of those who experience the consequences of the prediction. The relationship between cues and the behaviors they are used to anticipate can be viewed as a 2 X 2 set of contingencies. Four outcomes of a forecast are conceivable, whether or not intuitive seers are aware that their work can be thus evaluated. Figure 4.1 is a schema illustrating the bets given by any prognostic device. The "cutting points" need not be symmetrical as they are drawn in this figure. The diagram only illustrates the fact that judgments from cues involve four kinds of bets. These four outcomes indicate the relative probabilities of two kinds of correct decision and two kinds of incorrect decision:

Figure 4.1 Predictive Possibilities

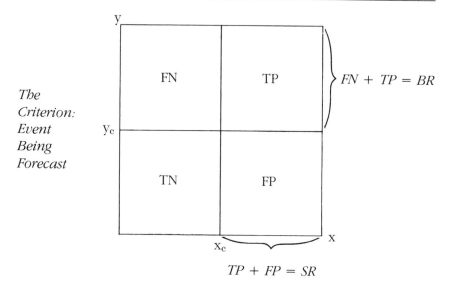

Test Scores or
Other Assessment Procedures

x_c = some cutting point above which one predicts "yes" and below which, "no."
y_c = the cutting point classifying the events being forecast.
FN = false negatives   TP = true positives
TN = true negatives   FP = false positives
BR = base rate   SR = selection ratio

1. *The probability of true positives,* written P(TP): The test or the judge predicts that people who score above a certain point, or who exhibit certain characteristics, will do Y, and they do.
2. *The probability of true negatives,* P(TN): The test predicts that such people will *not* do Y, and they do not.
3. *The probability of false positives,* P(FP): The test indicates that such people will do Y, but they do not.
4. *The probability of false negatives,* P(FN): The test says that they will not do Y, but such people do.

The probabilities of each of these four possible outcomes is determined for a particular sample of acts and actors by dividing the numbers in each cell by the total number in the sample. The power of a forecasting instrument can then be measured. The measurement involves several dimensions.

A test, or a judge's assessment procedure, is *sensitive* insofar as it correctly identifies people who commit the crime we are forecasting. Sensitivity = P(TP).

A test is *specific* insofar as it correctly identifies people who will *not* commit the crime we are forecasting. Specificity = P(TN).

A test's *predictive value* is the percentage of *positive* identifications—of murderers, for example— that are accurate when the test is applied to a population that contains both murderers and non-murderers. The predictive value of a positive bet

$$= \frac{P(TP)}{P(TP) + P(FP)}$$

The job of a forecasting tool is to improve upon a guess that would be made by knowing only the *base rate—BR*—of the event being predicted in a particular population. The base rate is the proportion of those people who actually commit the crime, or exhibit the behavior, that is of interest. BR = TP + FN. It consists of our accurate hits plus our wrong predictions about people who do Y when we have bet that they would not.

Judgment of future action also involves a decision about "where"—beyond what score—to anticipate that people are likely to do the acts of interest. This cutting point defines the *selection ratio: SR*. It is the proportion of a sample judged to be likely to commit the crime we are predicting and it includes, of course, our correct and incorrect judgments. SR = TP + FP.

BR and SR are important because they limit the degree of association that can obtain between any set of cues and the events being forecast. By definition, a test, or other judgmental procedure, will be perfectly accurate if, and only if, SR = BR. But, as SR and BR diverge, as the difference between their probabilities increases, accurate decisions become less frequent.

The *utility* of applying a test—that is, of using any set of indicators of the likelihood of the events of interest—is a matter of relative costs. The relative costs are values, or "utilities," assigned by decision-makers to the proportions of true positives, true negatives, false positives, and false negatives produced by a prognostic instrument.

Each of these four bets carries a price. Estimating that price, and willingness to pay it, vary with the kind of event being forecast and with those involved in the decision. For example, in medical diagnosis one aspect of the price is the amount of damage judged to be associated with correct and incorrect diagnosis of a disease. And the actors in the decision drama are physicians, patients, patients' families, and, sometimes, concerned citizens. In criminal cases, different values are assigned to the judged gravity of particular categories of crime. And the actors involved are those experts asked to make predictions, judges and juries, offenders, their victims, and concerned citizens.

To employ any predictive device in public situations is to engage in a difficult balancing act among diverse actors who make different assessments of the relative utilities of the bets provided by that device.

The *expected utility, EU,* of a decision made through the application of any set of cues is a function of the *values* assigned the bets in each of the four cells of a prediction table, *multiplied* by the *probabilities* of each outcome. Summing these products, and subtracting the cost of making the decision, provides a strategy by which to maximize the expected utilities of decision processes. The cost of making the decision includes such expenditures as inventing a test, applying it, or holding a staff conference to decide an issue. This cost must be subtracted from the net gain of our correct and incorrect bets. The relationship between expected utility and the values and probabilities of the four kinds of outcome is written:

$$EU = \Sigma \ U_i \cdot P(O_i) - U_t$$

Value is emphasized in this equation because the cost of a decision is not just a matter of accuracy versus inaccuracy. It is also a matter of how much the two kinds of accuracy/inaccuracy are worth to the person who is deciding or to persons who are affected by the decision.

Implications

In assessing attempts to predict behavior, two facts deserve emphasis.

The first fact is that predictive statements based on experience tables are always statements about statistical probabilities, not certainties. And this means that they are statements about the *relative frequency* with which *kinds of people* do kinds of acts or they are statements about the *relative frequency* with which an *individual* does particular things categorized as X. In both cases—that of singling out dangerous individuals in a heterogeneous population and that of foretelling what an individual will do—statistical probability refers to relative frequency and this requires counting. The tallies of events that appear in the numerator of a probability statement must be related to some base. Statistical probability denotes a *relationship*. As we shall see (page 87), the base from which we predict can vary, and comparisons made from different population bases are improper.

In the work of identifying dangerous individuals in a large population, the base of the rate is all the people. In the work of anticipating what a particular individual, and we ourselves, are likely to do, the base of the rate is all activities, usually partitioned in units of time. Judgments of ourselves and others, whether they be everyday opinions or expert ones, combine, in some non-mathematical way, estimates of the future from an individual's past and judgments of the individual from his/her similarity to some subset of a population with an estimated frequency of doing X.

One point of this comment on probability is that it is incorrect to judge the power of a predictive instrument from single instances of success or failure. It is incorrect to expect all-or-none forecasts, such as "she will or she won't." It is incorrect to equate the fact of her act with its probability before the event. It is true, after the fact, that she either did it or didn't. But in *pre*-diction, we have only probabilities to work with. We know one another, and ourselves, only from propensities, likelihoods of doing this or that. And the fact that what we do is more and less probable means that it need not be only this and never that.

An additional reason for commenting on "probability" is to note that his word has more than one meaning (Hacking 1975, von Mises 1957). However, the notion of *statistical* probability refers to relative frequency and this idea can only operate by relating something *actual* to a base of people or events or situations that have the *potential* of exhibiting whatever is counted in the numerator. This means that probabilities *change* with changes in the base of people or events against which the acts of interest are compared.

A second fact follows: It is easier to invent tests that improve our predictions as the base rates of the events being forecast approach 50 percent (Meehl & Rosen 1955). By contrast, as events become more rare or more frequent in a population, it becomes more difficult to invent tests that have predictive value. This is the case, of course, in trying to identify dangerous persons in a population that includes a wide assortment of people with varying dispositions toward violence. In the identification of such rare individuals, or in the forecast of such unusual events, *tests of modest validity will increase the proportion of wrong bets!*[3]

Summary

Our excursion over the costs of decision illustrates a point that is commonsensical, but often forgotten: *That every predictive decision prices the value of accurate judgment against the cost of mistake.*

The cost of mistake is, in turn, of two kinds: Betting that he will attack, but he does not, and betting that he will not attack, but he does. The price paid for these mistakes is subjective. It is a matter of the values (utilities) assigned to the two kinds of erroneous prediction and the two kinds of correct prediction. These two dimensions of decision, *probability and value,* are inescapable components of judgment.

We try to reduce the costs of decision by knowing something and by thinking straight. But, given uncertain knowledge in a hazardous world, every decision carries its cost. The advice given in Volume One, Chapter 3, to look for continuities and to bet on them is an attempt to reduce the price paid for decision. The utility of that advice will be demonstrated by epidemiological research and by an illustrative tragedy (following pages), but it is first necessary to comment on the populations for which predictions are made.

POPULATIONS AT RISK

By definition, accurate indicators of future conduct are those that identify people who constitute the base rate. The easiest way to increase accuracy is to *refine* the rate from which a prediction is made. To refine a rate is to *narrow* the population base so that it includes *all those people and only those people at risk* of doing whatever is counted in the numerator.

---

[3] A common source of error in judgment derives from *ignoring* base rate information. "The base rate fallacy is people's tendency to ignore base rates in favor of . . . individuating information . . . rather than integrate the two" (Bar-Hillel 1978, p. 1).

Considerable experimentation demonstrates that judgment is distorted by information that seems somehow "relevant," specific or causal, and which dominates knowledge of base rates (Kahneman & Tversky 1973, Tversky & Kahneman 1980). In such cases, even though seers may be confident in their judgments, the "relevant" information from which they estimate probabilities *reduces* the accuracy of their bets.

Now, as a rate is refined—as the population base becomes more se-lect—it becomes more difficult to identify an individual within this smaller pool who will, or won't, commit the crime in which we are interested. Our best bet is simply to forecast that everyone in such a thinned-out population will do so.

In sum, we approach limits in our ability to refine rates, using de-mographic data, biographies, test scores, or any combination of such cues. It is difficult to make a refinement upon forecasts from base rates *if* a population is relatively homogeneous with respect to the events being studied. If violence is either rare or frequent within a population, it becomes a tough job to invent a set of cues that im-proves predictive power beyond that given from a base rate estimate.

It follows that any statement about the relative success or failure of experts or instruments in predicting danger is only as good as the population for which it is made, with specification of its base rate of violent activity and the selection ratio used to identify the violent actors.

These facts affect interpretation of research on the efficacy of fore-casts of dangerous conduct. For example, Steadman and Cocozza (1974) followed the careers of patients for three years after they were released from a high security hospital for the criminally insane—the "Baxtrom" patients, so titled after the legal decision that released them. The patients' record of violent behavior was compared with that of a control group of psychiatric patients judged to be non-dangerous. On five measures of violent activity, including sub-sequent arrest for violent crimes, no significant difference was found between the two classes of patient.

Unfortunately, this finding is difficult to interpret because age and sex differences are obscure. Furthermore, Gordon (1977) shows that it is possible to identify a dangerous group within the Baxtrom popu-lation. He writes:

> When the sample released into the community was divided according to both age and score on [the] Legal Dangerousness Scale . . ., it was found that patients less than 50 years old with a score of 5 or more were dis-tinctly more dangerous than the rest. Within this subgroup, 47.2 percent had been arrested and 30.6 percent had been involved in violent assaul-tive acts [with an average time at risk of 2½ years] (p. 216).

Different populations and different instruments give different re-sults. Thus Wenk and Emrich (1972) studied the careers of 4,146 men paroled from the California Youth Authority (CYA) at an average age of 19.4 years. Only 6 percent of this sample had been incarcerated for a violent crime, and breaches of parole for violent offenses for the entire sample during the 15 months at risk was only 2.25 percent. However, it is possible to improve upon this forecast by identifying subgroups more likely to be violent. Thus young men who had been referred for psychiatric evaluation of their violent disposition exhibited a higher arrest rate (6.2 percent) on parole. So did men with a prior record of violence (5.2 percent), or four or more prior sentences to the CYA (4.8 percent), or a violent crime as the instant offense that sent them to CYA (4.8 percent). Later development of a prediction instrument increased hit rates to 14 percent of parole violators (Wenk, Robison, & Smith 1972).

The CYA studies yield a high rate of false positives for a low rate of accurate identification, and it is this kind of finding that leads some writers to say that danger cannot be predicted.

However, another set of estimated risks has been produced from a different population. Kozol, Boucher, and Garofalo (1972) studied the careers of 592 men who had been convicted of "serious sex offenses," half of which involved violence or its threat. At an average age of 35.6 years, 435 of these men were released under varied dispositions. Psychiatrists diagnosed 304 of these men as *not* dangerous and they were released after serving their sentences without referral for further treatment. Of these "non-dangerous" men, 8.6 percent were arrested for violent crimes within five years of their release.

Psychiatrists also diagnosed 131 of these men as dangerous and recommended their indefinite confinement in a mental hospital. The court rejected 31 of these diagnoses and released what it believed to be these false positive cases. Thirty-nine percent of this group was later arrested for violent crimes, one of which was a murder. An additional 18 men were released after an average of 30 months' treatment, but again contrary to psychiatric judgment that these men continued to be dangerous. Twenty-eight percent of this group was later convicted of violent crimes, one a murder.

Yet another population of select offenders yields higher rates of recidivism. Koppin (1976) charted the careers of 111 men found not guilty of felonies by reason of insanity, but released conditionally at an average age of 33 years after serving an average of 4.5 years. Their release was based on psychiatric opinion that they were no longer dangerous.

Within 2 to 4 years after their release, 42.3 percent were arrested. Thirty percent were arrested for violent crimes, defined as physical assault or its "serious" threat. Koppin shows that it is possible to refine this rate by creating a sub-population of men under the age of 50 years who score 5 or higher on the Legal Dangerousness Scale. Among this more select group, 66.7 percent were arrested, 48.3 percent for "violent" offenses.

Significance

These few investigations demonstrate the variety of accurate and inaccurate forecasts to be expected when different populations, varying in size, age, sex, and biography, are diagnosed as dangerous by a variety of instruments and diagnosticians.

It is also to be noted that none of this research *prices* the probabilities of the forecasts, failed or successful. Given the quality of crimes committed, the estimated probabilities by themselves cannot inform decision. What has to be added is a judgment about the *values* of hits in each of the four cells of a contingency table (Figure 4.1).

It will be argued (pages 95–98) that it is easier for an individual to price these probabilities for his/her own use than it is for any expert to price them for public policy. In the case of "social choice," conflict is inevitable between the interests of potential victims and defenders of the rights of falsely identified dangerous persons.

This conflict does not readily dissolve with information because it is a moral quarrel, one concerning justice. While moral arguments are important, they do not lend themselves to resolution with the tools of rational decisionmaking. Gordon (1977) describes the difficulty in the context of imperfect predictions of dangerousness:

> To the extent that individuals are truly different, treating them as equally dangerous raises questions of justice that tend to override all other considerations. Much of the force of the rhetoric of "false" positives and "innocent men and women" derives from the high priority we accord to justice in our society in combination with the presumption that the false and true positives really were profoundly different from each other at the start despite our not being able to tell them apart. In short, justice appears to be a quality with "infinite utility." Because they make a shambles of decision theory, qualities with this property are usually excluded from analysis. It is easy to understand, then, why even relatively modest false positive rates, such as those obtained by Kozol et al., can be brought under heavy fire (p. 234).

Gordon is correct. Nevertheless, those who have moral doubts seek more information on which to base their judgments. Some of this information comes from epidemiological research that shows us how better to refine rates and when to count on continuity.

Epidemiology and Continuity

Epidemiology is defined narrowly as "the branch of medicine deal-ing with epidemic disease" (*Random House Dictionary of the English Language* 1966). More broadly, epidemiology is the study of the dif-ferential distribution of activities among populations and areas. The value of such research is to suggest causes of the events that interest us by noting differences in rates of these occurrences among different kinds of people in different "ecological niches." The search for causes proceeds by successive refining of rates as per the procedure described in Volume One, Chapter 3.

Epidemiological research can tell us something about the bound-aries within which we may expect to find continuities. This mode of analysis indicates who are more likely to be carriers of qualities of violence.

Rabkin (1979) has reviewed epidemiological research designed to answer questions about the criminal activity of discharged mental patients. Since the public fears the "mentally ill," the question of their dangerousness persists. Rabkin analyzes results from five Ameri-can studies conducted between 1922 and 1955 and compares those results with findings from eight studies conducted since 1965. She re-ports as follows:

1. Today and over the past 20 years, mental patients discharged from public facilities *as a group* have total arrest rates for all crimes that equal or exceed public rates with which they have been compared. Arrest and conviction rates for the subcategory of violent crimes were found to ex-ceed general population rates in every study in which they were mea-sured. (p. 21, emphasis hers).

2. The arrest rates of paroled and discharged patients based on pre-1950 records consistently were found to be lower than those reported for the general population. There has been a pronounced relative as well as absolute increase in arrests of mental patients since then; that is, whereas arrest rates for both patients and the general public have increased, the rate of acceleration for patients has been much greater. (p. 21).

3. [Two factors account for this increase: Quicker release of mental patients and the hospitalization of "disturbed" offenders who previously would have been jailed.] Today in New York State facilities as elsewhere, the average patient stay is 30 days. In acute-care units, patients are usually discharged within 2 weeks (p. 22).

4. It has been repeatedly and convincingly demonstrated that the small subset of patients who have prior criminal records accounts for a large majority of postdischarge arrests. This is the *single best predictor* so far identified. . . .

Other predictors, which are significantly associated with postdischarge arrests but not large in their effect, include male sex, youth, and unmarried status (p. 23, emphasis added).

5. At present one may conclude that patients with diagnoses of personality disorders, alcoholism, and drug dependency have disproportionate arrest rates (p. 23).

6. It was an unpleasant surprise to learn not only that patient arrest rates were the same or greater than those of the general population in recent years but that this excess was particulary pronounced in the category of felonies, and specifically, of violent crimes or crimes against persons. . . . The magnitude of this excess ranged from 1½ to 29 times greater than general population rates. No studies reported contrary findings. . . . It seems reasonable to conclude that mental patients are more likely to be arrested for assaultive and sometimes lethal behavior than are other people (p. 24).

7. In summary, reported recidivism rates for arrests among discharged mental patients range from 19 percent to 56 percent. These rates were derived from different periods of record surveillance, include different crime categories, and were gathered over a period of 30 years. In contrast, only 2–4 percent of patients without prior arrest records were arrested within 5 years after discharge. This analysis of recidivism rates reinforces the conclusion noted earlier that a history of prior arrests is a useful predictor of arrest risk after discharge (p. 25).

8. At the present time there is no evidence that their mental status as such raises their arrest risk; rather, *antisocial behavior* and *mentally ill behavior apparently coexist,* particularly among young, unmarried, unskilled, poor males, especially those belonging to ethnic minorities. It is unlikely that most people would care to have such neighbors even in the absence of a history of psychiatric hospitalization (p. 25, emphasis added).

9. When patients with arrest histories, primary diagnoses of substance abuse, and personality disorders are considered separately, the remainder of the patient group appears to be considerably less dangerous than are those members of the general public who are not mentally ill (p. 26).

Rabkin's findings are in conformity with some segments of public opinion (Piasecki 1975). Failure to believe in continuity in such careers leads to tragedy.

Gambling With Continuity

Four days after he was born, Troy Boothman was taken from his parents when other mothers in the hospital complained that Troy's 18-year-old mother, Louella, hit the infant for hurting her during breast-feeding.

Louella, an uncontrolled epileptic, had been in special classes since Grade 3, suffering from what were called "emotional problems" and unable to complete ordinary elementary schoolwork. She took some vocational courses, but could not "stand the pressure" of a job. In 1978 she was sent to Alberta Hospital, a "mental institution," where she remained for one year.

During her residence in hospital, she met another patient, Edmond Garth Boothman, who had been sentenced to psychiatric supervision in 1977 for the attempted murder of his brother. Garth had a history of violent outbursts that culminated in the attack on his brother. In ths brawl Garth stabbed his brother 11 times, breaking the blades of two knives and ending the fight with scissors. He was deemed not guilty because insane. A psychiatrist testified that his violence was caused by "irreversible brain damage." Garth was pacified in hospital with medication and discharged in 1980 on the promise that he would continue to take his medicine.

Louella and Garth married, but neither was capable of work. On the day they married, they had 60 cents between them and borrowed money from their wedding guests to pay for their marriage license. Garth also borrowed money from his future mother-in-law to buy a wedding ring and then pawned the ring for spending money.

Louella's parents reported to welfare officials that the couple often had no food because they had spent their social assistance checks on toys for themselves. Their rent went unpaid, yet they bought childish games, a tape deck, and a cassette player.

During the three months that their son, Troy, was a ward of the government, Louella and Garth petitioned family court in Edmonton to have their baby returned to them. In May, 1980, a social worker and a community health nurse recommended to the court that Troy be returned home under their supervision. The judge said he believed that "the problems in hospital had been overcome" and all those involved in the case assumed that "parental training" and counselling would assure a peaceful domestic scene.

When he was 14 weeks old, Troy was released to his parents and killed by his father the same day.

In the hullabaloo following publicity of this murder, the Director of Social Services asked, "How do you ensure that a tragedy will not occur? How far do you go? What is good supervision? I'm not sure what else we could have done, other than play it safe."

Louella's mother added, "Maybe with a little more guidance, maybe things could have worked out fine."

The leader of the Provincial socialist party added his predictable assessment: "The government should improve social worker training, raise wages to a competitive level, [and] increase staff." He also recommended removal of the Director of Social Services.

Persistent Errors

Such recommendations and other popular opinions expressed in response to this killing reveal persistent common errors. Correcting these errors requires recognition that:

1. Psychosis and imbecility are not "problems" that have "solutions." Psychosis and imbecility are terms that refer to biological statuses of neurochemical origin. Differential adaptation to these conditions varies with environment, of course, but it is foolish to assume "solutions" via "guidance."

2. Social workers are not people-changers. Counselling and instruction are ineffective remedies of temperament and cognitive deficit.

3. Judges, psychiatrists, and social workers are not accurate prognosticators. They have no expertise in the prediction of human behavior.

4. The political recommendation following such homicide is irrelevant. Increased funding of "social services" and reduced case loads of social workers will not prevent such tragedies. Unless a social worker is to baby-sit each incompetent set of parents, more social work is not a preventive.

5. Psychiatrists do no better at predicting violent behavior than do experience tables (Ennis & Litwak 1976, Monahan 1972, Tanay 1979). That is, psychiatrists add nothing to the prognosis made from base rates, where these are known, or from the record of violence in an individual career.

For example, Cocozza and Steadman (1976) studied how psychiatrists arrived at judgments of "dangerousness" among 257 indicted felony defendants in New York state. These investigators found that the single, significant predictor of a psychiatrist's judgment was *the gravity of the offense charged* against the defendant. However, this cue was mentioned by only one-third of the psychiatrists in their reports to the court. The predictor that they most frequently mentioned was "delusional or impaired thinking."

This finding confirms other research that reveals a discrepancy between *the actual cues employed* in psychiatric prediction and the cues that are *named* (Steadman 1973, Weinstein 1964). Such results remind us that *reasons* given for acts are not to be confused with the *causes* of those acts (see Volume One, Chapter 2).

A special Task Force of the American Psychiatric Association (1974) acknowledges this unfortunate "state of the art":

> Neither psychiatrists nor anyone else have reliably demonstrated an ability to predict future violence or "dangerousness." Neither has any special psychiatric "expertise" in this area been established (p. 28).

6. Last, cases like that of the Boothmans remind us that if reproducing is deemed to be everyone's "right," child abuse is a probable price of the privilege.

CONTINGENCIES AND MANY ROADS

We have described three difficulties in predicting danger: That of defining it, that of estimating the relative probabilities and values of correct and incorrect forecasts, and that of specifying the population within which a forecast is made. Predictions remain difficult for a fourth reason: That the dangers that interest us may be variously produced.

Although we count on continuity, we recognize that all bets are contingent. Much depends on "other things" happening, or not happening, and these other things are beyond our ken.

The fact that estimates of the future can only be probabilistic reflects the fact that the events we wish to foresee are contingent. These facts in turn confirm the possibility that many roads lead to similar destinations.

Difficulties of foretelling danger point to differences in public and private policy.

PERSONAL AND PUBLIC POLICY

Public policy is one thing; private policy is another. It is easier to devise rational policy for an individual than it is to devise a rational policy for a society. It it easier for two reasons: (1) individuals more frequently "know what they are doing" than do societal engineers because individuals experience the consequences of their acts, and (2) while individuals operate with mixed motives and hence may suffer "internal conflict," conflict is more apparent, and probably greater, among the objectives of social policy.[4]

Given, then, that all decision incurs the price of probable error, and given, in particular, the high proportion of false positive predictions made in the forecast of violent acts in a non-select population, social policy is difficult to formulate for free and heterogeneous societies. We have difficulty protecting ourselves against violent people by social policies that are to function under the laws of free states. The best that social policy can do is to quarantine the violent ones *after* their violence.

By contrast, personal policy does not suffer such constraint. For the purpose of individual protection, a high rate of false positive bet about dangerous others is justified by some hit rate of true positives and by the value assigned to freedom from injury.

What rates of correct and incorrect predictions justify protective strategies depend upon individual convenience, emotional bonds, and the value assigned to a beating. For example, lovers typically accept a *higher probability* of attack from their loved ones than from strangers. In the loving situation, this is justified by the possibility that a history of violence and present signs of danger may nevertheless yield a false positive prediction. This hope is then bolstered by moving the *source* of danger from the brutal loved one's disposition to his or her situation. Loving hope shifts the location of causation from "the way he is" to "the pressure he's under."

In addition to moving the source of danger, individual convenience and emotional ties place different *values* upon the probabili-

----

[4] A popular belief holds that information, organized as knowledge, will reduce conflicts in social policy. This premise is not always false, but it suffers from a tendency to assume uncritically that the answers knowledge gives will be the answers we want to hear.

We are returned to a theme expressed in Volume One, Chapter 1—that of the possible conflict between Truth and Utility. Knowledge does not guarantee the success of *preferred* policies. Such information may say "nay" as well as, or more often than, "yea."

Moreover the information that justifies our doing *this* to get *that* often tells us nothing about side-effects—about what will happen as we move from *here* to *there*. Thus students of "policy analysis" point out that government programs always have unintended consequences, that "one problem always succeeds and replaces another," that failure is "confronted" by changing what one is *supposed to accomplish* into what one *can do,* that plans are "nowhere fulfilled," that "theories [tend] to harden into dogma," and that "no one . . . has the knowledge to predict sequences of actions and reactions across the realm of public policy" (Wildavsky 1979, pp. 5–8).

This does not mean that "nothing works," but rather that little in the public arena works as promised.

ties—tallied or guessed—of false positive, true positive, and false negative bets. Our advice is to add predictive weight to behaviors that
betoken dispositions.

On "Disposition"

"Disposition" to act is an inference derived from observed behavioral continuity. The idea of "disposition" is a familiar one in medicine and, by analogy, its use in psychology can be clarified.

In the medical sense, a "disease" is a disturbance of proper function for which a specific cause has been identified. However, in medical philosophy, a specific cause is not everything that is *sufficient* to
produce the illness. It is only that which is *necessary*. Thus one cannot have a disease called "syphilis" without presence of the spiro-
chete and one cannot have "tuberculosis" without presence of the
tubercle bacillus, but not everyone whose body is invaded by such
organisms runs the same course or the full course of these diseases.
The necessary agent does not always produce the full-blown disorder, nor does it fix the career of the disease, and it may not be the
most important factor to be attacked in treatment.

We noted earlier (Volume One, Chapter 8) that physicians use the
word "diathesis" to refer to those constitutional differences that
make individuals more and less immune to disease. In similar fashion
it is advisable to employ the idea of disposition as a personal variable
mediating, if not overriding, the impact of situation upon conduct.

Every intuitive judge of others makes dispositional attributions.
What we debate is their relative acuity and predictive utility. *We become more sure of a dispositional attribution as we observe similar
acts by the same actor under varied circumstances.*

Without this opportunity, we extrapolate from those we have
known to those we are meeting. Extrapolation rests on generalization, and the everyday generalizations with which people operate
have been called "stereotypes." Social psychologists who employ
this term—one borrowed from journalism—have uncritically assumed
that stereotypes must be false, whereas the few tests of their validity
show that they may be more true than false (Volume Two, p. 53).
However, there is no escape from generalization and, if there is a risk
of error in "stereotypy," it is a risk common to all conception
(McCauley et al. 1980).

When we study those who bet their lives on the accuracy of their
assessment of dangerous people and situations, we find that the process by which they deduce danger is complex and multidimensional,
but that inferences about personal dispositions are central. For example, Rozelle and Baxter (1975) conducted interviews with 51 po-

lice officers in Houston to ascertain how they recognize danger. While there was some variation among personnel with different work experience, all officers assume enduring personality traits as cues with which to predict conduct. However, in assessing danger, officers widen the range of signs they employ and include situational cues as well as personality traits in their judgment.

CONCLUSIONS

We can improve the accuracy of our predictions by tallying base rates of violent behavior for segments of the population—kinds of people—who exhibit different propensities to attack.

Once we have segregated a group of violent actors high on a measure such as the Legal Dangerousness Scale, the best bet we can make is to regard them all as equally dangerous. To repeat, refining forecasts is uneconomical once one has identified a select population with extremely high, or low, base rates of the activity we are foretelling.

The importance assigned to predictions depends not only on the values attributed to probabilities in the four cells of a contingency table, but also on the *range* of probabilities that we have tallied from our experience with classes of actors and their deeds.

Events that have absolutely low probabilities may still assume importance if they represent upper or lower limits of some range of possibility of the events that interest us. Gordon (1977) illustrates the point with an analogy from baseball:

> . . . it is impossible for an ignorant but intelligent foreigner to determine from the absolute level of the probability alone whether a .333 season batting average is good or bad, although he could easily tell that it is only half as good as one of .666. But .666 does not occur as a season batting average. The range of interest of many phenomena is found to lie within only a very narrow segment of the probability continuum, and that segment often contains probabilities that are unimpressively low in absolute value. Batting averages, for example, typically range only between .2 and .4 How could our ignorant foreigner know that a mere 097 probability of hitting a home run described Babe Ruth in his greatest hitting season? Similarly, probabilities for individuals committing dangerous crimes within three years may seldom range higher than .3 to .5 in our society. When the probability becomes higher than that, it may apply to extremely unusual phenomena, such as armed desperadoes on a killing rampage. . . . In short, if we inquired into the matter, we might find that probabilities that appear modest in absolute value actually describe the Babe Ruths of dangerousness, and that it is unrealistic to ex-

pect values ever to get any higher than that. When they do, the societal reaction may be to shoot first and ask questions later. What this means, then, is that if society is ever to protect itself routinely against individuals that it experiences as the most dangerous of all, it is going to have to do so at probability levels between .3 and .5 or not do it at all (pp. 235-236).

Some people are more dangerous than others. There *are* individual carriers of violence. Signs are to be read by counting continuities in conduct. All such tallies are imperfect and, when they are used to forecast rare events in general populations, they produce errors as a price of their accuracy. This makes social policy difficult. But it provides guidance for personal policy. Individually we can afford many incorrect predictions of danger—false positives, but *not* false negatives—for the value provided by correct predictions.

The trade-off is of this nature: We recognize that most loaded guns do not go off accidentally and kill people and that most grizzly bears do not attack human beings. It would be foolish to argue, therefore, that loaded guns were not "dangerous" and that grizzly bears were no more potentially lethal than, say, rabbits.

So, too, with people. Not all persons loaded with hostility are triggered, any more than guns are. But safety lies in taking care with loaded guns, grizzly bears, and violent actors.

5 DETERRING

Abstract • Deterrence refers to the inhibition of likely action. ○ Individual deterrence is the hypothesis that people inhibit those acts that have had, or might have, painful consequences. • General deterrence is the hypothesis that punishing miscreants causes other possible offenders to resist temptation to commit the punished crime. • Individual deterrence is a contingent effect. ○ The effect varies with qualities of pains. ○ The effect varies with individual differences in appreciation of pain. ○ The effect varies with schedules of punishment. ○ The effect varies with group support of individuals. ○ The effect varies with individual experience, as per a contrast effect. ○ The effect varies with plan and impulse. ○ The effect varies with intelligence and with expected consequence. • Deterring individuals can correct them without "rehabilitating" them. "Threat therapy" is described. • General deterrence runs counter to the Kantian ethic. ○ The questionable morality of inducing general deterrence motivates search for justification in societal protection. ○ The search for such justification, conducted with poor instruments, has led some observers to conclude incorrectly that punishment can have no general deterrent effect. ○ "Fireside inductions" confirm the possibility of general deterrence. • Tests of general deterrence are described. ○ Three common assumptions underwrite such tests. ○ These tests have examined only certain pains, not all possible pains, for deterrent effect. ○ Tests of general deterrence have employed experiments, quasi-experiments, and analyses of uncontrolled variations "in nature." ○ Analyses of natural variations have proceeded cross-sectionally and longitudinally with inconsistent results. ○ Mathematical models testing for general deterrence are described. Their results are inconclusive. ○ Mathematical models suffer from poor data, uncertain decisions about what to include, from varied units of analysis, and from imperfect knowledge of the causal web in which crime rates are probably produced. 1. Causal webs are described as dense, sparse, or in-between. 2. Boundaries of a presumed causal system are often unknown. 3. Threshold effects are possibilities about which we know little. 4. Competing conceptions of causal style also affect confidence in mathematical models. ○ Models work with correlations, but the size of a correlation coefficient cannot be interpreted as a measure of causal power. • It is concluded that general deterrence remains everyone's plausible assumption even if its effect cannot be finely assessed. • It is also concluded that social policy in response to crime will be impelled more by what we want to do than by what the doing achieves.

MAGISTRATES AND CITIZENS ALIKE commonly justify punishing criminals by the presumed deterrent effects of pain. These effects have been partitioned into those experienced by the offender herself—an effect called *specific* or *individual deterrence*—and those experienced by others in the population who, although themselves unpunished, presumably know of the pains suffered by criminals and thus resist temptations to do as the offenders have done. The latter effect is known as *general deterrence.*

INDIVIDUAL DETERRENCE

Individuals *do* change their conduct as consequences of their acts change. There *are* individual deterrent effects and everyone assumes them. But there are also surprises as when punished individuals persist in their wicked ways despite the pains that follow their acts. It is crucial, therefore, to be able to specify which presumed punishment is how painful for which miscreant with what consequences. In short, we need to know the contingencies of inhibition.

Earlier discussion described some of these contingencies (Volume One, Chapter 6). Contingencies refer to the conditions that affect the possibility of protecting society by channeling the conduct of bad actors through pain. A review reminds us of the costs of trying to redirect most criminal careers through the official imposition of punishment.

1. Punishment is not one kind of event.

Pains vary in quality. Those that we impose on disapproved actors range from the stimulation of shame and guilt, to loss of money and freedom, to physical injuries and psychic deformations.

2. Individuals vary in the amount of pain they suffer from apparently similar quantities of punishment.

There *are* sadists and masochists, and individuals are differentially sensitive to the various styles of punishment. One can even become immune to pain. For example, in the Russia of Peter I (Peter the Great, 1672–1725) torture was common. Massie (1980) reports that:

> [The Russians'] incredible hardiness and unconquerable endurance of pain astonished not only foreigners but also Peter himself. Once, after a man had been tortured four times by knout and fire, Peter approached him in sheer wonder and asked how he could stand such great pain. The man was happy to talk about it and revealed to Peter the existence of a torture society of which he was a member. He explained that nobody was admitted without first being tortured, and that thereafter promotion within the society rested on being able to accept higher grades of torture. To this bizarre group, the knout was nothing (p. 251).

3. Schedules of pain and pleasure change consequences for actors.

Schedules include *timing* and *intensity* of pleasurable and horrible experiences and the relative *balance* of these experiences in a shifting course of conduct.

A weakness in punishing offenders in order to change their behavior is that the presumed pain imposed comes long after the anticipatory cues leading to the bad act and the pleasure of that act. Tardy punishment is relatively ineffective. Early punishment is most effective. Punishment as the tempted actor moves toward his crime would be even more effective, but it would, of course, be unjust even were it possible.

4. Group-supported miscreants feel less pain from the same presumed quantity of punishment.

There *are* martyrs.

5. Punishment is more effective when it is a contrast effect than when it is a constant experience.

Punishment administered by a usually rewarding agent is more painful than punishment administered by a commonly punitive agent.

Ostracism of a gangster by the "family" that has been his principal source of satisfaction and self-reference is more painful than shaming and blaming by a "correctional" officer who represents another "tribe" that has never rewarded the mobster.

Conversely, kindness given to one who has been repeatedly punished may also provide a motivating contrast effect. This effect has been less well documented and it may not be as powerful an effect as rare punishment administered by a normally loving guide. A possible cause of this relative impotence is that persistent punishment damages an individual's trust and sensitivity to kindness. Nevertheless, this kind of contrast effect is sometimes reported. Massie's history notes:

> More astonishing and even touching was the fact that sometimes the same Russians who could withstand the knout and fire and remain mute until death would break if handled with kindness. This happened with the man who told Peter of the torture society. He had refused to utter a word of confession although he had been tortured four times. Peter, seeing that he was invulnerable to pain, walked up to him and kissed him, saying, "It's no secret to me that you know about the plot against me. You have been punished enough. Now confess of your own accord

out of the love you owe me as your sovereign. And I swear, by the God who has made me tsar, not only to completely pardon you, but in addition, as a special mark of my clemency, to make you a colonel." This unorthodox approach so unnerved and moved the prisoner that he took the Tsar in his arms and said, "For me, this is the greatest torture of all. There is no other way you could have made me speak." He told Peter everything, and the Tsar, true to the bargain, pardoned him and promoted him to colonel (p. 252. Reproduced by permission of Random House, Inc., publishers. © 1980 by Robert K. Massie).

6. Punishment inhibits planful action more readily than it inhibits impulsive behavior.

We acknowledge that "plan" and "impulse" represent end-points on a continuum of activity and that careers are running mixtures of planned and spontaneous action. Nevertheless, the efficacy of a deterrent depends on the health of that planning agency called "the mind," located principally in the brain. Therefore, brains that are addled with "comforting chemicals"—chronically or periodically—are not effective guidance mechanisms subject to control by conceivable consequences. Earlier pages (Volume Two, Chapter 3; Volume Three, Chapter 4) noted the high proportion of "textbook crooks" that has been disabled by alcohol and other disinhibiting agents. Among American armed robbers, "drugs and booze" are prominent, both as motivant for their crimes and as stupefying factors that reduce the rationality of their work. Petersilia and her colleagues (1978) report that, among their habitual California felons, two-thirds regularly used "comforting chemicals" and 60 percent were under the influence of alcohol or drugs when committing their crimes.

7. Inhibition is easier as the probability of punishment comes closer and is more credible.

To put it the other way about, more people lie, cheat, and steal, the easier it is to get away with a broken rule (Volume Three, Chapter 1). Social science cannot specify *thresholds* of temptation for individuals or aggregates, or for situations and kinds of crime. Nevertheless, both research and common sense confirm that, "When the cat's away, the mice will play." Individual inhibition is made easier by the "presence of the cop."

James Press (1977) tested this possibility when one New York City police precinct—the 20th—increased patrol personnel by 40 percent—from an average of 212 to 298 men—while patrols elsewhere in the city remained constant. Press collected data from the 20th precinct and some other precincts in the city that had had similar patterns of crime. He then analyzed crime reports for the three years preceding the "experiment" and for 14 months thereafter, adjusting the reports for seasonal variation and testing net changes in reported crime per week for statistical significance.

He found that the change in police power reduced those crimes that were "visible from the street," while it did not affect "hidden" crimes. Table 5.1 gives Press's results:

Table 5.1 Changes in Crime Rates of "Inside" and "Outside" Crimes*

ROBBERY	A net decrease of 2.6 crimes per week (33%) for crimes visible from the street and a net decrease of about 2 crimes per week (21%) for others.
GRAND LARCENY	A net decrease of 17 crimes per week (49%) for crimes visible from the street and a net decrease of 6.6 crimes per week (29%) for others.
BURGLARY	Changes in reported crime not visible from the street (97% of all burglaries in New York) were not statistically significant.
AUTO THEFT	There was a net decrease of 7.7 crimes per week (49%).
MISCELLANEOUS FELONIES	There was a net decrease of 1.9 crimes per week (38%) for crimes visible from the street.
TOTAL FELONIES	A net decrease of 23.7 crimes per week (36%) for crimes visible from the street and a net decrease of 4.4 crimes per week (5%) for others.
MISCELLANEOUS MISDEMEANORS	Crimes visible from the street showed a net decrease of 8 crimes per week (15%); other crime changes were not statistically significant.
TOTAL MISDEMEANORS	Net changes were not statistically significant.

*"Outside crimes" = those visible from the street; "Inside crimes" = those not visible from the street (Reproduced with emendations from S. James Press, "Police manpower versus crime," In J.M. Tanur et al. (eds.), *Statistics: A Guide to Political and Social Issues.* © 1977 by Holden-Day, Inc., and reprinted by permission of the publisher).

These findings demonstrate some individual deterrence, but they do not price the relative costs of increased policing and reduced crime.

8. Punishment and its threat work best as inhibitors of bad actors who perform their misdeeds solo, who have normal or better intelligence (which is also to say, whose minds are not chemically muddled), and who have more to lose in the promised punishment than they have to gain from the pleasures of their crimes. Individual deterrence varies with expected consequence.

Correction ≠ Rehabilitation

Punishment, then, changes individuals. When it produces inhibition of their crimes, we may say that they have been corrected. This style of correction is often contrasted with the vague ideal of "rehabilitation."

To rehabilitate means to re-build. Technically rehabilitation refers to restoration of an organism to health or of an edifice to its former beauty. This assumes, of course, that there was once a healthy organism or an intact edifice that can be reconstructed.

Corrections—and in particular change through pain—does not restore; it alters. In many criminal cases, this is a desirable objective.

"Threat Therapy"

Individuals change their activities as *their* appreciation of consequences changes. Allowing for the contingencies we have discussed, this effect can be induced *if* future pain is made credible along with an intervention that breaks a current course.

In illustration, Murray and his associates (Murray and Cox 1979, Murray et al. 1978) developed a program known as UDIS—"Unified Delinquency Intervention Services." With an annual budget of over $2 million, their Chicago office took referrals of chronic bad actors, those who ordinarily would have been sent to juvenile detention facilities. These boys, and some girls, had "more than a dozen arrests, half a dozen appearances in court, and three temporary detentions" (1979, p. 34).

The UDIS plan was to suppress future criminality with a roster of services administered by "vendors" under contract.

> The vendors might be private or public agencies, store-front operations, church groups, school-related institutions, or . . . they might offer counseling services, educational or vocational training . . . or residential pro-

gramming in group homes or in foster care. Note that UDIS was not exclusively community-based; it also established contracts with a number
of out-of-town residential placements such as wilderness programs, the
Work Camp . . . and intensive care services in psychiatric facilities (1978,
p. 3).

Murray and his colleagues tested the deterrent effect of this intervention for boys against a baseline of their delinquent activity for the
four years prior to program entry compared with delinquent activity
for 18 months after the program. They also made a comparison between such careers among the UDIS boys and those sent to residential detention centers under the Department of Corrections (short-
hand, DOC).

The important findings are these:

1. Both UDIS and DOC "had a powerful and apparently long-term
inhibiting effect on subsequent delinquent activity" (p. 4).

Police records for the year after intervention compared with police
records for the year before showed, for UDIS and DOC combined, a
reduction in arrests of 68 percent, in court appearances of 46 percent,
of "violence-related" offenses of 74 percent, and of "aggregate
seriousness costs" of offenses of 65 percent.

2. A two-year follow-up revealed stability of these effects.

3. Suppression of criminal activity does *not* mean that these boys
did not repeat crimes. They did. In accord with the usual statistics on
youthful recidivism, 60 percent of UDIS and 69 percent of DOC boys
were arrested again within a year of their "treatment." However, the
quantity of activity—the *offense* rate rather than the *offender* rate—
was apparently reduced.

4. Suppression works without "solving boys' problems," "curing
psyches," or improving abilities.

UDIS employed what Glasser (1965) calls "reality therapy" and
what might more accurately be called "threat therapy." DOC was a
back-up threat, a promise of pain if the boy did not control his
behavior.

The promise was embedded, however, within a context of sympathetic guidance. Intensive intervention got boys' attention, listened
to boys' stories, and made real for them an inventory of options, including the awful option of being "put away" if they continued in
their depredations.

5. An option such as UDIS costs the community. It costs but little
more in dollars than incarceration, but it costs the community much
more in crimes committed while boys are "free" in the program.

For every eight boys who stayed in UDIS for the typical eight-month period, one was apprehended during that time for an armed or strong-
armed robbery. One of every eight was arrested for assault or battery. For
every four, one was arrested for burglary. For every 48, one was arrested
for homicide (p. 23).

6. Comparisons between UDIS and DOC are not possible because
presumably more dangerous offenders were selected for institutionalization.

In summary, individual deterrence works, but it works im-
perfectly. Its effects are bent by contingencies that are beyond the
control of correction in free societies. Therefore, programs like UDIS
are not cures, but they may be options in the graduated steps with
which a criminal justice system responds to youthful crime.

An Illustrative Case

Individuals are more easily deterred by "threat therapy" when
they are solo predators, intelligent, and uncontaminated by "dope."
"Faggotty Freddie" illustrates the point.

Schoolmates had attached a moniker like this to Fred (his real title
is protected) because at eight years of age he began homosexual attacks on smaller boys. The attacks included verbal and physical abuse
and humiliation of victims forced to submit to Fred's sexual
urgencies.

The town in which Fred lived had a forensic clinic that worked
with psychoanalytic assumptions. Fred was deemed to be "acting
out" hostility that was caused by maternal rejection. His parents and
younger sister were involved in family therapy that was to expose
the source of Fred's disorder, produce insight, and thus relieve the
"symptom," aggressive homosexuality.

Fred's sexual attacks persisted. When he was 17 the family moved
to another city at great expense and principally because Fred's teen-
age sister was ashamed to go to school where Fred, and she in turn,
were objects of ridicule. It was also hoped that a move would change
things.

Fred found new victims in his new city and was soon referred to a
clinic whose psychologists operated with less dogmatic assumptions
than those of psychoanalysis. During the course of first meetings with
Fred, he was arrested for a crime that had not been in his repertoire—
exhibitionism.

The series of examinations and consultations that had been started
allowed a psychologist to "report" findings to Fred. He was told by
the counsellor in whom he now had confidence that the report was

to be interpreted factually, rather than morally, just as though Fed were being told his height and weight. Fred understood. He was then told that he was a homosexual.

The effect was electric. Fred claimed that in his years of psychotherapy no one had told him this.

The psychologist validated his diagnosis by describing in vulgar detail how Fred *felt* when he exposed himself and attacked boys. The description fit and Fred assented to it.

Fred was then told that he was of normal intelligence and not "crazy." He eagerly agreed with this diagnosis.

The psychologist added that to be sane—not crazy—means:

> You can control youself. You don't have to bugger young boys or wave your masculine pride at strange ladies. However, if I'm wrong—if you can't control yourself—then you *are* crazy and the court may decide to put you away.

In graphic detail, and in language Fred could *feel,* the psychologist described what would happen to Fred "the next time, the very next time, you even say 'shit' to someone." He was given a grisly picture of the court's options and of the likely victimization of Fred himself under these options. He was also given clear instruction about what to do with his sexual appetite that would not get him in trouble.

In this case, threat therapy worked, at least for the four years during which the counsellor was kept informed. However, the threat was embedded in a context of concern so that Fred believed he had a friend with whom he could discuss, as he put it, "What's going to happen to me."

Scared Straight

A highly publicized effort to apply threat therapy took potential and actual juvenile delinquents to the Rahway State Prison in New Jersey where "lifers" gave them tough talk about the pains of prison.

In the first six months after this experience, a comparison of the criminal activity of the threatened boys with that of a control group showed an apparent "deterioration effect"—the threatened youths committed more crimes (Finckenauer 1979). However, Langer (1981) noted that a majority of the exposed boys had no police record. When he compared the criminal activity of boys who had been arrested prior to the threatening experience, he found that their known delinquencies remained relatively constant during 22 months after exposure to tough talk while the control group had increased its criminal activity. Moreover, the effect of threat therapy became more pronounced as the juveniles who were "scared straight" approached the age at which they could be sent to prison as adults.

In summary, threat therapy works, but it works best when the threat is real rather than merely promised. We repeatedly observe individual deterrence, but we acknowledge that it operates contingently. However, individual deterrence is easier to justify and to observe than general deterrence.

GENERAL DETERRENCE

The German philosopher Immanuel Kant (1724–1804) developed an ethical system that holds that it is always wrong for one person to use another as an instrument. Kant's second formulation of his famous Categorical Imperative commands:

> So act as to treat humanity whether in thine own person or that of any other, in every case as an end withal, never as means only (1972, pp. 46–47).

This is a difficult commandment to follow since all human connections can be said to continue or dissolve as a result of an "exchange" of satisfactions.[1] Other people, in actuality, then become means as well as ends-in-themselves, whether or not we regard them so. Kant's ethic is therefore narrowed by some philosophers to prescribe only that one person or group should not "use" another against the other's "will." And "against her will" then comes to mean without the "used" person's knowledge or consent.

However, whether or not we approve of Kant's ethical mandate, societies *do* use some people as instruments with which to influence others. This is particularly the case when the law imposes pain on one bad actor in order to reduce temptation for others. This use is justified as providing societal protection through general deterrence. Given the questionable morality of this employment, at least for Kantians, attention has been directed to tests of the necessity and efficiency of styles of deterrence.

---

[1] Georg Simmel (1950, p. 387) claimed that "all contacts among men rest on the schema of giving and returning the equivalence," and more recent theorists have attempted to generalize "exchange theory" (Blau 1964, Homans 1961).

While it seems useful to regard continuing "to know one another" as a function of values received and prices paid—particularly if these are broadened beyond material costs and benefits to include psychic ones as well—"exchange theory" runs the hazard of explaining everything *after the fact* with a set of tautologies (Heath 1976).

Common Sense and Academic Theory

Common sense and sociopsychological research have a history of conflict. A good reason for studying behavior scientifically is to test popular generalizations; some of them are false. A good reason to be skeptical of behavioral science is that it is vulnerable to generalization beyond its facts where the facts themselves are drawn from soft data with weak instruments.

The question of general deterrence is one of the most difficult questions, perhaps *the* most difficult one, put to criminologists. We have not been able to give it a clear answer. But psychologists and criminologists have contributed to the wrong conclusion that no deterrent works. Today many journalists and other lay persons state dogmatically that "Punishment does not deter" and, more specifically, that "Social science has proved that capital punishment does not deter homicide."

The best answer to these dogmatic assertions is that they are true, false, or unproven depending on where, when, and how styles of punishment are applied and tested. Common sense assumes that, under some conditions, some pains administered to *others* for particular acts inhibit *us* from similar actions. The effect is especially demonstrable at extremes—at the extreme of license where "everything is allowed" and at the extreme of reliable repression where "everything that isn't forbidden is compulsory" (Malaparte 1964, p. 203).

Fireside Inductions

Paul Meehl (1977) calls commonsensical generalizations "fireside inductions," meaning that both individual experience and historical interpretation verify the belief, for example, that the plausible threat of severe consequences inhibits action. Meehl notes that:

> The same psychologist who says punishment does not deter relies on deterrence in posting a sign in the department library stating that if a student removes a journal without permission, his privilege to use the room will be suspended but his use fee not returned. This same psychologist suspends his children's TV privileges when they fight over which channel to watch; tells the truth on his income tax form for fear of the legal consequences of lying; and drives his car well within the speed limit on a certain street, having been informed that the police have been conducting speed traps there. It will not do for this psychologist to say that as a citizen, parent, professor, taxpayer, automobile driver, he must make such judgments upon inadequate evidence, but, when contemplating the legal order, he must rely only on scientific information.

> Psychologists and psychiatrists says strange things when pressed to document their statement that the criminal law cannot deter. They say, for example, that the only way to control behavior is to get at its source or origin, rather than penalizing it; that capital punishment has been shown not to deter murders; that experimental research on the behavior of infrahuman animals has demonstrated that punishment is an ineffective mode of behavior control. These are the three commonest responses, along with a general overall flavor to think about crime "scientifically" instead of "in moralistic categories, e.g., *justice*" (p. 12, emphasis his).

For the citizenry, their own experiences and those related by others confirm that painful consequences change behavior. Meehl observes that:

> Law enforcement officers cannot get into the higher echelons of the drug traffic because the small-fry peddlers cannot be effectively pressured by a prosecutor to tell anything about the next level of the higher-ups. Peddlers have a solid conviction, amounting to a subjective certainty, that if they are known or strongly suspected to have turned stool pigeon, they will be killed by the organized narcotics underworld (p. 15).

At the extremity of probable and severe punishment, tyrannies work. They work, and have worked, in Fascist, Nazi, and Communist dictatorships where civilized persons, transformed into subjects, learn not to speak freely to their visiting relatives from Canada and the United States. The fact that there are rebels, martyrs, and other exceptions does not invalidate the generalization. Exceptions "prove" rules only in the Latin sense (*probare*) of testing them: Too many exceptions, not much rule. But generalizations, by definition, are statements that allow exceptions.

Repression works, but its efficiency, like that of all methods, is contingent. In illustration, Meehl comments on the quelling of the French mutiny during the bloody battle at Verdun in which two million men were engaged and one million killed:

> We have a fairly clear case in connection with the mass insubordination, defection, and mutiny of the French army during World War I. In 1917, following the collapse of the Nivelle offensive, morale in the French army was desperately low. The constant danger of death or horrible wounds, the obvious pointlessness of the attacks, and the overall conditions of daily existence must have provided a set of psychological instigations whose pervasiveness, intensity, and duration were beyond anything found in civilian life. In some units, refusals to obey orders had the full character of a mass mutiny and over half of the French army's divisions

experienced such mutinies. In the Ninth Division, all three regiments formed a protest march in which they sang the *Internationale* and shouted, "We won't go up the line!"

Petain, who had replaced Nivelle, understood the instigations to mutiny and took appropriate steps to see that some conditions (e.g., insufficient rest between attacks) did not occur. But he also recognized that the currrent emergency situation, in which half the army was mutinous, required drastic summary treatment. "I set about suppressing serious cases of indiscipline with utmost urgency [Barnett 1965, p. 237]." Verdicts of guilty were passed on over 23,000 men, i.e., 1 in every 100 men in the field army on the Western front. Only 432 were sentenced to death and only 55 of these were actually shot, the remainder being sent to penal settlements. But, of course, every soldier and officer knew that the new commander was determined to punish mutineers, and the tiny number of executions were carefully dispersed and widely publicized. The general deterrence notion in criminal law presupposes knowledge or, more precisely, belief as to sanctions. As Petain wrote, "the High Command [must impress] on all ranks that it is resolved on the strictest discipline and obedience. . . . It must ruthlessly make examples where necessary and bring them to the knowledge of the army [Barnett 1965, p. 226]."

As the fireside inductions would predict, the mutinies ceased entirely and immediately. Presumably the efficacy of Petain's approach lay in some near-optimal combination of (1) reduced instigations to mutiny, or the hope thereof, under new command; (2) severity of the penalty; and (3) near certainty of detection (p. 14).

Fireside inductions about general deterrence gain credence as we observe the effects of a loss of police. Without exception, removal of the police means at least a short-term outbreak of violence and looting. This is particularly notable in revolutionary times, but it has been dramatically recorded whenever police have gone on strike or have been incapacitated. For example, during World War II, invading Nazis arrested the entire Danish police force and left only an unarmed constabulary to enforce the law. Crime rates increased ten-fold (Radzinowicz & King 1977, p. 150).

Police strikes are consistently followed by orgies of destruction. Looting continued for several days when half the Liverpool police struck in 1919. The strike of Montreal police in 1969 produced carnival vandalism in the central business area and a dramatic increase in burglaries, muggings, and bank robberies (Clark 1969). Looters invaded major downtown stores, attacked the U.S. Consulate and McGill University, and rioted against symbols of "The English Establishment." Rioters killed one person and wounded 49.

Looting is also an expected consequence of power failures in urban centers when police are diverted and incapacitated. For the general public, repeated experiences such as these confirm a belief in general deterrence without the necessity of quantifying that effect. Social scientists, of course, try to count it.

Tests of General Deterrence

Social scientists have endeavored to specify the contingencies under which kinds of pains inhibit tempted actors in a population that may not have experienced the pains themselves, but that believes them to be probable. Volumes have been written about these efforts (Blumstein et al. 1979, Cousineau 1976, Gibbs 1975, Zimring & Hawkins 1973). Here we need only summarize the research assumptions, modes of measurement, and some reasonable conclusions.

Assumptions

Three commonsensical assumptions underwrite research on general deterrence:

1. That people are moved by the conceivable consequences of their acts.

2. That people evaluate consequences by a process that appreciates jointly the possibility of discovery and the quality and severity of probable punishment if caught.

3. That the citizenry at large has some awareness of the legal liabilities of committing kinds of crimes.

Pains Measured and Omitted

Not all punishments that might deter, and do deter, have been studied in a criminal justice context. The pains most frequently noted are arrest, conviction, fine, incarceration, and execution. Pains that have been considered, but poorly assessed, include those of restitution, community service order, and probation and parole supervision.

Pains that have been disregarded in research outside the laboratory—that is, in "real life"—are those powerful fears of shame and stigma—of what Goffman (1963) calls "spoiled identity." These punishments seem considered, however, by some people tempted to commit crime and by people who evaluate the justice of response to crime.

Methods

Three methods have been proposed and variously employed to weigh general deterrent effect: Experiments, quasi-experiments, and analyses of uncontrolled variations "in nature."

Experiments are seldom conducted outside laboratories and, in such controlled situations, ethical considerations limit the scope of the experiment. Far more experiments have been conducted on individual deterrence than on general deterrence, with some of the results summarized on pages 102–106.

Quasi-experiments refer to changes in presumably significant causes that are *not* within the control of the observer, but that are identifiable within some limited time frame. For example, quasi-experimental tests of general deterrence examine the effects of changes in laws upon kinds of crime. A difficulty with some research employing this procedure has arisen from mistaking a change in the law for a change in imposition of a punishment. It is the error of confusing law-on-the-books with law-enforcement.

This confusion characterizes some early research on the effects of capital punishment that led to the incorrect conclusion, repeated in several textbooks, that the death penalty did not deter murder. Peck (1976) and Ehrlich and Mark (1978) criticize this confusion in Sellin's (1959, 1961) attempts to assess the impact of capital punishment.

Quasi-experimental procedures also analyze the effects of changes in styles of punishment and changes in law enforcement as in campaigns against speeding or impaired drivers (Ross 1977). This procedure has been used, too, in testing for homicide rates after execution of a murderer (Dann 1935, Graves 1967, Phillips 1980b, Savitz 1958).

The best conclusion from the better controlled research is that highly publicized penalties have at least a short-term generally inhibiting effect. A difficulty with inducing long-term effects is that punishment has to be kept credible; it must be enforced. This effort costs something in personnel, vigilance, and the psychic price of inflicting pain. Hence, states often relent after an episodic deterrent campaign. Nevertheless, even homicide, ordinarily considered to be so heavily impulsive as to be beyond deterrence, can be *momentarily* inhibited by publicized, painful consequences.

Momentary Inhibition

Phillips (1980b) studied British vital statistics for 1858–1921 and noted *weekly* variations in homicide just prior to, during, and following 22 well-publicized executions in London. His study is more sensitive to possible deterrent effects than the usual research on this topic that examines *yearly* variations in homicide correlated with capital punishment. Such a long span can conceal short-term deterrent effects.

Phillips finds that homicide rates declined by 35.7 percent during the week of a widely publicized execution and for one week thereafter. But within two to five weeks after the execution, homicide rates increased above their normal level so that a "stability of killing" is apparent.

Phillips' study has no relevance for public policy since such a short-term, compensated effect cannot be used to justify executions. The research does indicate, however, that a general deterrent effect is possible.

The most frequent test of general deterrence records changes in crime rates that occur "naturally," that is, without the intrusion of some purposeful change in laws or their enforcement. This kind of test looks for changes in crime rates correlated with changes in the frequency and severity of some imposed pain, with or without time-lag.

Correlation analyses of "naturally" fluctuating crime rates have proceeded in two ways: Cross-sectionally and longitudinally. A *cross-sectional* analysis measures differences in crime rates and punishment levels among different jurisdictions during the same period. A *longitudinal* study evaluates a time series, that is, it notes changes in crime rates followed by variations in punishment, followed by changes in crime rates, and it records these movements over a number of years within one jurisdiction.

Confidence in social science would increase if cross-sectional and longitudinal research gave the same result. Unfortunately, these procedures yield conflicting findings in sufficient cases as to call caution to betting on their predictions. This is true of research on deterrence as it is of other studies of motivation. Thus Klein and his colleagues (1978, p. 342) report that discrepancies between time-series and cross-sectional analyses also appear in econometric models of consumer spending:

> In national time-series samples [of consumer spending], there is evidence of significant positive association, at the margin, between an index of consumer attitudes and spending on durable goods; but in cross-section samples, with family-to-family variation, this same effect cannot readily be found. . . . It has also been the case that significant time-series effects have not always carried over from sample to extrapolation.

Our interpretation of such inconsistency is, again, that one cannot leap directly from observed correlations to causal conclusions. Pages 120–121 will specify additional sources of error in deriving predictive bets from correlations alone, even when the correlations are manipulated in complex models.

Mathematical Models Again

Recent years have seen the importation of mathematical models, largely from economics, into investigations of general deterrent effects. These models have the advantages of making researchers clarify their assumptions and of evaluating a host of factors presumed to produce some effect. Their results may have the additional advantage of silencing the dogmatic assurances of professional debaters on the punishment question.

These models proceed by running off correlations between the event of interest—a crime rate, in our case—and a number of variables presumed to cause that event directly or indirectly. Thus models of "the production of crime" have analyzed the relation between rates of a "kind of crime"—robbery or homicide, for example—and some or all of such punitive contingencies as:

$P(A)$ = probability of apprehension (e.g., clearance rate or arrests per crime)

$P(C)$ = probability of conviction (e.g., convictions per crime)

$P(J)$ = probability of trial (e.g., trials per crime)

$P(I)$ = probability of imprisonment or other custodial handling (e.g., prison commitments per crime)

T = severity of punishment (e.g., time incarcerated)

$P(E/C)$ = probability of execution, given conviction

Cop = a measure of intensity of police presence (e.g., police expenditures per person or police per person)

PrExp = prison expenditure per prisoner

Holding constant some or all such indirect causes of crime as:

Y = median income

MC = proportion of population that is middle class

Pov = a measure of poverty or of income dispersion (e.g., percent of families with incomes below $3,000)

NW = a measure of racial composition (e.g., percent non-white or percent AmerIndian)

Un = a measure of employment opportunity (e.g., unemployment rate or labor participation rate)

Age   = a measure of age composition (e.g., percent of the population between 25 and 35)

Sex   = a measure of sex composition (e.g., sex ratio: males per 100 females)

N   = total population

Den   = a measure of population density or housing density

Urb   = a measure of urbanization (e.g., percent of population living in SMSAs [Standard Metropolitan Statistical Areas])

So   = a measure of the southern regional variable

Ed   = a measure of educational level (e.g., median years of schooling of the population over 25 years old)

Prop   = a measure of property values (e.g., assessed property value per capita)

Mig   = migration rate

NHW   = proportion of households that are *not* husband/wife households

Temp   = average temperature

Rec   = number of households with record players

Car   = motor vehicle registration per capita

Price   = average price of new cars

MuEx   = municipal expenditures on recreation, education, etc.

Tot.mun   = total municipal budget

Tax   = per person property taxes

t   = time

Gov   = government expenditures per person

City size = geographical area of city (sq. miles)

[This list has been reproduced with some emendations from D. Nagin, "General Deterrence: A Review of the Empirical Evidence." His Table 1. In A. Blumstein et al. (eds.), *Deterrence and Incapacitation: Estimating the Effects of Criminal Sanctions on Crime Rates.* 1978. Reproduced with permission of The National Academy of Sciences, Washington, D.C.]

Researchers who have constructed such models of crime production sometimes are bold enough to make predictive statements out of their findings, statements such as these:

> ... the empirical analysis suggests that on the average the tradeoff between the execution of an offender and the lives of potential victims it might have saved was of the order of magnitude of 1 for 8 for the period 1933–1967 in the United States (Ehrlich 1975, p. 398).

> ... the combined effects of a $500 increase in income would probably be a reduction of about 5.2 arrests per 1,000 population. In areas of high

tendencies toward crime, a 10 percent rise in incomes might well result in a 20 percent decline in delinquency (Fleisher 1966, p. 117).

If our analysis is correct, a 10 percent increase in the probability of being arrested will result, other things being equal, in a 5 percent reduction in the rate of serious robberies (Wilson & Boland 1976, p. 201).

Of course, other things are never equal and such assurances have not gone unchallenged. What one econometrician discovers, another refutes. Nagin (1978) reviewed over 20 attempts to gauge mathematically the general deterrent effects of punishment. He concludes that:

Despite the intensity of the research effort, the empirical evidence is still not sufficient for providing a rigorous confirmation of the existence of a deterrent effect. Perhaps more important, the evidence is woefully inadequate for providing a good estimate of the *magnitude* of whatever effect may exist.

The development of public policy directed explicitly at crime control is dependent upon sound estimates of the magnitude of deterrent effects. Thus, policy suggestions, based upon the existing evidence, can only be made with a clear recognition of the inadequacy of the evidence (pp. 135–136, emphasis added).

Brier and Fienberg (1980) draw similar conclusions from a later review of the economic modelling of crime and punishment. They believe that "little or no progress has been made during the past 10 years in our understanding of the potential deterrent effects of punishment on crime" and that there is "no reliable empirical support in the existing econometrics literature either for or against the deterrence hypothesis" (pp. 95–96).

In sum, despite the apparent elegance of mathematical models of crime production, they offer little practical advice beyond that available to reasonable intelligence. The practical impotence of these computerized pictures lies in their inability to isolate the impact of one alleged cause or set of causes upon events, like crimes, that are probably produced in a dense web of causes. The effort is much like trying to weigh a fly on truck scales.

For present purposes, the major difficulties of testing for general deterrence with mathematical models can be outlined without elaboration:

1. Mathematical models are as good, or bad, as the quality of the measures put into them. Computer "jockeys" have a slogan, "Garbage in, garbage out."

As we have seen, measures of real crime rates are crude and so are tallies of the distribution of criminal activity in a population and of the actual and subjectively appreciated risks of punishment.

2. Models vary in what they include and exclude. Some of the plausible causes of variations in criminal activity are omitted because they cannot be well gauged.

3. Models vary in the units of analysis they employ.

The assumptions underwriting research on general deterrence (p. 114) refer to individuals. That is, individuals are the alleged recipients of the message sent by punishment of others. However, most individuals do not live alone, bereft of social influence, and we may expect a different result if the unit of analysis is the family or neighborhood rather than the individual.

What is at issue is the "ecological fallacy," again, or "aggregation bias" (Volume One, p. 64). This is the possibility that the shape of an association between two or more variables may change as the unit of analysis changes.

While the sociopsychological assumptions of the general deterrence hypothesis refer to individuals and, perhaps, to larger "living units," most of the research testing for the deterrent effect has used aggregated data—data grouped for a city, state (province), region, or entire country. And, without discussing *how* this comes to be, it is a statistical fact that different results can be achieved by computing correlations using different levels of analysis. For example, Greenberg, Kessler, and Logan (1981) show that some discrepancies arise when identical models of crime production employ city data rather than state data. These investigators tested the mutual effects of crime rates and probabilities of arrest using information from 98 American cities for 1964–1970 and all 50 states for 1964–1968. While both data sets indicate no effect on index crime rates with marginal changes in probabilities of arrest, they differ in estimating the effects of crime rates on probabilities of arrest.

The mathematical models probing for possible general deterrence have not been "well-specified," which is to say that the data used have not been the kinds of data indicated by the "theory" to be tested.

4. The web of causes in which crime is generated is unknown.

Causation is a context-bound idea. In Volume One, Chapter 8 we noted that we can conceive of systems of causes that are densely packed and full of changing interactions, or as sparsely structured with a few causes having strong, non-contingent effects, or as something in-between.

In response to crime, the punishments that are presumed to affect crime rates may themselves be the effects of those rates. Blumstein and Cohen (1973), Blumstein, Cohen, and Nagin (1977), and Blumstein and Moitra (1979) demonstrate a possible interaction between crime and punishment such that punishment "seeks" a stable level. According to this hypothesis, if crimes increase beyond some level, punishment decreases because of system overload. Conversely, if crime decreases beyond some level, punishment increases to "fill the system."

However, the present point is not concerned with the validity of a "homeostatic theory of punishment." The point is that the *independence* of a nominated cause cannot be assumed. The entire system of causes moves. Effects "feed back" upon what were once causes and become causes themselves. Reality does not hold still so that a mathematical model can describe it well enough for predictive purposes. If the world worked that way, econometricians would be rich from anticipating the movement of markets.

Difficulties with weighing causes that operate in systems are briefly these:

1. We are not certain of the *boundaries* of the causal system. Events deemed to be outside the system may, in some fluctuating way, invade it. "We cannot be certain," said an astrophysicist, "that the flutter of a moth's wing may not precipitate a hurricane."

2. Relevant to (1), we can only guess at, and sometimes test for, *threshold effects.*

Causes that are apparently inoperative up to level-alpha may become operative as they cross the threshold into level-beta. Cumulating causes can be hidden. Moreover, thresholds can change as the entire system changes.

What is required if we are to cross a deterrent threshold for particular quantities and qualities of crime may be beyond our powers or our wills.

3. We can only guess at, and sometimes test, competing conceptions of *causal style.*

"Style" refers here to assumptions about whether causes *add* impetus one to another, or whether causes have *multiplier* effects, or whether some causes have additive effects while others have multiplicative effects. Furthermore, if there are multiplicative effects, we do not know their magnitudes, and correlations won't reveal them.

We do not know how much weight to assign nominated causes and whether, as the system changes, the weights also may change. On this point, *the degree of association*—the size of a correlation coefficient—*cannot be interpreted as a measure of causal power.*

Only controlled experiment can provide estimates of causal powers. Lacking that, we rely on imperfect judgments formed out of personal experience modified by the vicarious experience gained by reading research reports and history.

Conclusion

General deterrence cannot be denied, even though it cannot be finely weighed. At some juncture, everyone believes in general deterrence, even if its operation cannot be accurately portrayed. Research that was to have informed judgment on this subject has been of little help.

A modern idea that motivates research is that facts can make public policies more efficient. The idea has some validity; most of us accept it in a vague way, particularly insofar as we prefer to think of ourselves as rational. However, it seems fair to conclude that social policy in response to crime will continue to be impelled more by what we want to do than by what the doing achieves.

This conclusion applies as well to the justification that some response to crime corrects offenders, the topic of the next chapter.

6 CORRECTING OFFENDERS

Abstract • Correcting offenders is usually distinguished from deterring them. ○ A distinction concerns the imposition of pain. ○ Some therapies are painful, but they may be distinguished from "punishment" if they are not intended to express resentment. ○ Nevertheless, a "tyranny of treatment" is conceivable. • Attempts to change people include magic, religion, force, and a variety of psychotherapies, behavior therapies, somatotherapies, and chemotherapies. ○ Magical curing is defined. ○ Psychotherapy by psychoanalysis, encounter groups, and the "honesty" treatments are described. ○ Deterioration effects are possible. ○ Behavior therapy differs from psychotherapy in de-emphasizing talk and reason and emphasizing changes in the consequences of acts. • Adequate assessment of results must satisfy seven research requirements. ○ Most research in evaluation of correctional procedures do *not* satisfy these requirements. ○ The conclusion that we do not know "what works" is challenged. • It is concluded that we have no balance-sheet on the efficacy of the therapies, that there is no *science* of corrections, and that it does not matter how well correctional efforts work *if* they have no worse effect than other responses to crime and can satisfy justice.

CORRECTING OFFENDERS is a popular reason for responding to crime. Correction has sometimes been called "rehabilitation," but that term, we have seen, is a misnomer.

The correctional justification is usually distinguished from deterrence. It is allegedly more "humane." The distinction between correcting offenders and deterring them is often more moral than practical since some individuals *are* corrected by threat and some *are* reformed by being punished. However, the objective of correcting offenders usually seeks to avoid punishing them. It tries, instead, to change actions by changing minds, teaching skills, or renovating environments.

Psychotherapy, Behavior Therapy, and Pain

The change of attitude that has been a perennial objective of movements to proselytize deviant people has been translated in modern correctional settings from religious conversion toward people-changing efforts known as the psychotherapies.

Psychotherapy is distinguished from other modes of reform in that it operates on the assumption that thinking, with its ally in feeling, controls action. On this premise, it is believed that changing thoughts will change behavior.

By contrast, behavior therapy, or behavior modification, assumes that it is easier to change actions by manipulating their consequences than it is to change actions by manipulating ideas. It is further assumed that as actions change, thoughts will change—a reversal of the causal schema of the psychotherapies.

An additional assumption that is voiced by psychotherapists, but less frequently by behavior therapists, is that their "treatment" is to be distinguished from punishment. Therapy can be distinguished from punishment *if* "punishment" is a term reserved for pains imposed to express resentment. However, it should be clear that many therapies are painful and that distinctions between psychotherapies, behavior therapies, and punishment get blurred in practice.

Tyranny of Treatment

Citizens are aware that treatment may be more painful than punishment, and they have been particularly suspicious of efforts to modify behaviors by changing the schedules of reinforcement in which potential and actual offenders function. For example, fear of "brain-washing" caused the American government to ban use of federal funds for behavior therapy of inmates. Prisoner-defense groups claimed that such reformation was a violation of convicts' rights. As a consequence, a prison that was originally called "The U.S. Behavioral Research Center" at Butner, North Carolina, had its name changed to "Federal Center for Correctional Research" and, later, to "The Butner Federal Correctional Institution."

Suspicion of correctional efforts is justified *if* lengthy intrusions upon others' lives substitutes for just response to their crimes. There is evidence that helpers who prefer to "treat" offenders rather than to punish or restrain them see more people in need of their "help" and favor longer detention of wayward persons (Cousineau & Veevers 1972, McNamara 1975, Szasz 1957, 1958, 1963, Wheeler et al. 1968, Wilson 1968). Outerbridge (1968) refers to the possibility of unjust intervention as "the tyranny of treatment."

One offender-addict, comedian Lenny Bruce (1972), reports his impression of the choice between being punished and being reformed:

> Thus the judge was making it possible for me to have, instead of two years in prison, 10 years of rehabilitation—if I'm eligible—based on the recommendation of two physicians appointed by the court.
>
> "Mr. Bruce, you're lucky. We're going to give you 10 years of help."
>
> "I don't deserve it really, I'm a rotten bastard" (p. 210).

Perennial People-Changing

Attempts to change people are as old as history. The principal instruments of change have been magic, religion, and force. Converting others to a "true faith" has been, and is, a justification for killing those who are reluctant. "Cultural revolutions" are always deadly.

To the ancient tools of persuasion, modern societies have added a wonderful inventory of devices. No previous tribes or civilizations have tried so many techniques or directed so much energy to reformation of conduct. In Western Europe and America north of the Rio Grande, helping others to change is a major industry. Incalculable sums are spent out of public and private funds to correct an expanding array of undesirable feelings and actions—from reading disability to unpopularity, from neuroses and psychoses to psychopathy and rational devotion to crime.

Not surprisingly, there is competition for the trade of treating behavior, and lawsuits flourish to determine who is entitled to payment as a legitimate therapist (American Psychological Association 1980, Kiesler & Pallak 1980).

All efforts at people-changing, ancient and modern, do some good. At least those who pay for the efforts derive some satisfaction for their money. All these efforts are also likely to do some harm. Evaluating these attempts is complicated by the intrusion of wish upon interpretation of result and by mixing the kinds of changes being assessed. Curing a phobia is one thing; correcting a way of life is another.

Some forms of correctional procedure require description before we look at attempts to measure their results.

EFFORTS

Parloff (1979) counts 130 modes of curing conduct. A recent handbook of psychotherapy (Herink 1980) lists alphabetically 250 brands of "cure" from "Active Analytic Psychotherapy" to "Zaraleya Psychoenergetic Technique." Therapies are recommended for individuals, couples, families, and groups. They are prescribed for short spans (a week-end of "est") and long periods (years with a psychoanalyst). Of all these therapies the oldest, most common, and perhaps most effective are magical.

Magic

"Magic" is used here as an exact and neutral term, not as a pejorative. Magic appeals to an unseen power that will work the cure. The practitioner of magic may claim special techniques for focusing the unseen power upon his patient, but the agency of the cure is outside the material world.

The appeal to unseen forces may be ritualized, as in an organized religion that defines faith healing as part of its justification, or it may be personalized, as when a particular individual is believed to have a special competence in using the spirit world to effect cures.

Magic is an accompaniment of all medical practice among preliterate people and it remains a prominent treatment among literate groups. It is often used in combination with physical therapy such as herbs, rest, massage, and hot and cold baths. Practitioners of magic, medicine men, undergo extensive training to learn the ceremonials of their people and, in some tribes, there is even a specialization of function between the diagnostician and the healer.

Demand for magical treatment in the United States, and elsewhere, has never been higher. To meet the demand, the American federal government has financed a training program for medicine men in Arizona (McDowell 1973).

The prominent philosopher-psychologist Karl Jaspers (1948) believes that a comparison of the results of faith healers and modern psychotherapists would prove the former more effective. Jaspers finds it "self-evident that the greatest success has been achieved, not by neurophysicians, but undoubtedly, as in earlier times, by shamans, priests, founders of sects, miracle-workers, father confessors, and spiritual leaders."

Psychotherapies

As the title denotes, psychotherapies are plural. They are linked by the assumption that changing thoughts and feelings will change actions. They run a gamut of procedures from counselling to exercises, but whether or not physical tasks are part of the treatment, a major objective is to give patients "insight" into how and why they behave as they do. The central premise is that "understanding" the sources of our difficulties relieves us of them.

"Understanding" in this therapeutic context does not mean "being able to say," or "having information," or "knowing" something. People who "know" things about themselves without appropriately changing their behaviors are said by their psychotherapists to have "intellectual understanding" but no "emotional understanding." The "understanding" that is sought, then, is more than "mere cognition" and includes the correlative emotions that are assumed to be both the object of the cure and the instrument for effecting it.

Since the principal tool of the psychotherapies is words, they have been derisively called "the talking therapies." They range, however, from pure talk to talk mixed with action. They include sympathetic listening and "undirected" appreciation of the client's "problem" as well as reasoning and persuasion—procedures that are near the counselling end of the spectrum. They also include analyzing "the games one is playing," either one-to-one with a therapist or in groups (Berne 1964), having patients shriek and throw things (Janov 1970, 1972), using forceful massage as a means of "breaking down the muscular armor" of neurotics (Reich 1973), insulting patients as a way of making them "face reality" (Stern 1972), and "loving" them via sexual intercourse (Wolf 1974). Psychologists used to call the last technique "penis therapy" until they learned of female therapists who have intercourse with their male and female patients.

Three of the many forms of psychotherapy have been particularly popular in Western lands—psychoanalysis, encounter groups, and the honesty therapies. They deserve brief comment.

Psychoanalysis

Psychoanalysis has been the most widely publicized style of psychotherapy. This long and expensive procedure requires the patient to recall memories of adolescence, childhood, and even infancy (Lindner 1944), and then to analyze what is recalled, along with other "freely associated" ideas, on the assumption that the patient will "work through" and resolve the presumed conflict between conscience and desire that has allegedly produced the unwanted "symptoms."

This method has been outlawed in some countries—in communist states in particular (Kiev 1968, Wortis 1950)—but it has dominated North American psychiatric training and practice. Wolpe (1981) believes that this school remains the dominant mode of training clinical psychologists. In the United States, the government agency responsible for spending millions of dollars annually to promote research and training in psychiatry, the National Institute of Mental Health, "recently had as its director someone who had been psychoanalyzed; the deputy director had been psychoanalyzed as well; and even the research director had been put on the couch" (Sargant 1964, p. 90).

It is an interesting commentary on the need to believe in the possibilities of reformation that this popular and costly "cure" has no demonstrable record of success (Rachman & Wilson 1980). In fact, one of the founders of this school, Sigmund Freud, believed that his invention was more of a research tool than a therapy. Freud himself reported the detailed therapy of only five patients and, by his own admission, some of these select few did not get well. The poverty of this procedure has moved the British psychiatrist Sargant (1964) to suggest that "Freud's work [in therapy] may be one of the great hoaxes of the century."

Encounter Groups

Encounter groups, also called T- (for training) and "sensitivity-training" groups, began in the late 1940s at an Episcopal Church retreat in Bethel, Maine. This procedure combines talk with some desensitizing experiences and group pressure. It assumes that:

1. Our difficulties result principally from inhibition and that improvement in human relations comes from honestly expressing our emotions.

2. "Opening" ourselves to our feelings and communicating them to others releases impounded talent and helps us become happier, healthier, and more "creative."

3. If we do not get along well with others, the trouble lies in our incorrect conception (usually called "perception") of ourselves. Such incorrect conception of self allegedly causes incorrect conception of others and leads to difficulty in "relating" to them.

4. Correct conception of self and others improves our conduct.

The "encounter" gathers people under the direction of a "facilitator" whose role is largely neutral but who may, in some sessions, serve as an interpreter for the group. Therapy calls for an "unfreezing" of old attitudes, acquisition of new views, and a "refreezing" or consolidation of these new images and values.

The group therapy proceeds by encouraging participants to tell what troubles them, to express their feelings about others in the group, and, depending on the style of encountter, to engage in desensitization experiences that range from verbal report of the unbearable to holding hands, feeling bodies, and nude group-grope in warm pools. A book in praise of this method is appropriately titled *Please Touch* (Howard 1970).

Encounter groups differ from the more traditional psychoanalytic group sessions in their employment of desensitization procedures and in the length of their meetings. T-groups often live together for weeks, meeting daily for two or three sessions of several hours each. Marathon encounters are sometimes arranged in which the participants remain together for an entire day or longer. For example, Church (1973) reports that the cosmetics and house-care company for which he worked urged him to sign up for a four-day course, at a fee of $1,000, in which the first session lasted thirty-nine hours.

This mode of therapy has been widely employed in prisons. It has also been adopted by business organizations as a means of increasing productivity, by government agencies as a technique for "sensitizing" bureaucrats, and by some judicial districts as a means of improving the quality of legal judgment.

Results

Good results may occur from acting on wrong premises—by chance, as we say—but it is more likely that incorrect assumptions produce undesirable consequences. There is no good reason to believe that much bad action is caused by inaccurate conceptions of ourselves and others or that correct conceptions reduce evil actions (Nettler 1961).

Yet, despite its poor working assumption, sensitivity training may do some good and we look for measures of outcomes. But, as with other forms of psychotherapy, *results* of this treatment are, to say the least, inconclusive. Participants' expressions of satisfaction are, of course, no measure of change in their conduct. Although more research has been addressed to assessing the effects of T-groups than any other management technique (Argyris 1964), it is difficult to get encounter enthusiasts to specify treatment objectives in concrete terms—an "'existential'" language is preferred. Thus, when Campbell and Dunnette (1968) reviewed research on encounter effects, they found that, although participants often *say* they have changed, improvement in job performance has not been documented.

To assess this and other therapies, one should calculate a *net score*. Psychotherapies are not without their costs, and one of the possible costs is a worsening of performance. There *are* "deterioration effects," as they are called, and allegations of improved conduct are fairly evaluated only after discounting for damage (Bergin 1971). In fact, Underwood (1965) finds that deterioration effects are more common among those who engage in encounter groups than among comparable others who receive no such treatment. Other investigators also report ugly encounters (Church & Carnes 1973, Odiorne 1963, Stafford 1973).

On Therapeutic Damage

Physicians recognize "iatrogenic" diseases. These are disorders caused by the treatment itself. If iatrogenic damage is possible in physical treatment, it is even more probable among efforts to change thoughts, emotions, and actions.

The possible range of deterioration effects produced by the many modes of psychotherapy and other correctional interventions has only been partly explored and need not be limited to the side-effects of "sensitivity" training.

For example, we have reports of therapists' domination and exploitation of their patients. Another form of damage is apparent in unnecessary, prolonged, and futile treatment. The case of the "family therapy" of "Faggotty Freddie" (Chapter 5) provides one illustration. Wechsler's (1972) account of the psychiatric treatment of his son is another example.

Ulla Bondeson's (1975) survey of 11 studies of correctional efforts in Denmark, Sweden, and Finland also suggests deterioration effects. She finds no reformative results of psychiatric or medical treatment or of educational and vocational programs, but she does note damaging effects upon both male and female inmates.

McCord (1978, 1980) gives an even more alarming report. She followed 506 men who had participated more than 30 years earlier in the famous Cambridge-Somerville Youth Study. She finds that the men in the treatment group, when compared with their matched untreated peers, fared worse.

The treated group suffer from a host of disorders. They have more trouble with alcohol and, consequently, with their jobs. They suffer more frequently from circulatory diseases. They have been divorced more often and report more dissatisfaction with their present marriages. Compared with their untreated coevals, the treated men have been disproportionately criminally recidivist and diagnosed as psychotic. Men in the treated cohort are also more likely to have died before age 35.

McCord cannot explain these possibly iatrogenic effects, but the only plausible cause she can suggest is that treatment raised men's expectations unrealistically and that this, in turn, induced a sense of relative deprivation not stimulated in the control group.

Even behavior modification, which is usually considered to be safe from deterioration effects, has been found to produce them under some circumstances. Thus Ross (1975) and Ross and McKay (1976) report that female adolescent offenders *increased* their criminal activity after behavior therapy.

Predictive Errors

Predictive mistakes are yet another kind of cost of intervention, and one that has not been adequately tallied. The very training and ideology of some practitioners contributes to their errors in prediction. For example, Sutherland's review of the practice of social work in England holds that:

> Social workers have not been conspicuously successful in saving battered children. . . . [one reason] is their naive faith in the importance of the relationships between the child and its biological parents. To judge by the number of cases in which children are forcibly returned from good foster-homes to the care of evil or negligent parents, this silly belief is shared by the courts.

Sutherland's comment applies in North America as well. The child-killing described on pages 93–95 followed a social worker's mistaken judgment.

Predictive errors of this sort result from disbelief in the probable continuity of conduct and from an unjustified faith in good intentions and the power of "communication." To employ social workers as prognosticators is to misuse their talents. Such use is now under challenge (Brewer & Lait 1980).

Honesty Therapies

Another style of psychotherapy counsels people toward a more realistic picture of themselves and their social environments. Hence, Glasser (1965) calls his treatment "reality therapy" while Ellis (1962, 1964) calls his approach, "rational psychotherapy."

The effectiveness of persuasion to rationality depends on the intelligence of the client, on the nature of the discomfort being addressed, and, of course, on rapport between the therapist and the inquirer. If confidence can be built, the therapist becomes more like a teacher than a physician of the emotions. The counselor assists clients in assessing their present situation and in weighing the probable prices of optional courses of action.

A considerable number of disturbed persons who ask for psychotherapy are neither neurotic nor psychotic. They are more frequently persons who are morally troubled. They are torn between liking-disliking what they are doing and confused by what others tell them they are doing and should do. They ask, in effect, for moral guidance. The "rational therapist" provides this, but usually in a relativistic context. The therapist shows the inquirer different moral definitions of the difficulties the patient is having. At this point, the troubled person frequently asks the moral question directly, "What should I do?" or "What do you think is right?" Help here lies in the counselor's having a morality that can be modeled.

This form of psychotherapy is of value only to those offenders who have been episodically delinquent, who are emotionally calm, and who ask for the help. It is of no value as a coerced therapy, imposed upon prisoners, and it is of little value to compulsive actors or to those who have rational grounds for persisting in a criminal career.

Behavior Therapy

Behavior therapy de-emphasizes cure by talk and reason. It attempts to alter conduct by changing the setting in which behavior is stimulated and reinforced.

This kind of therapy does not assume that the "deeper causes" of a patient's actions must be known or that the patient must come to "understand" the sources of his or her conduct. Behavior therapy has an advantage over the psychotherapies in that it works with explicit hypotheses about how people learn, hypotheses described in Volume One, Chapter 6.

Applying behavior therapy requires ability of the therapist—or the people he/she is instructing, such as parents—to control a schedule of reinforcement. That is, this procedure works only if a pattern of reinforcers can be put in place. When this can be done, and when the therapeutic target consists of a *limited* range of action, this mode of treatment has probably the best recorded rate of success among the therapies (Wolpe 1981)—with the possible exception of *voluntarily* elected, religiously oriented group processes, like Alcoholics Anonymous. Success is particularly apparent in the correction of phobias (Chapel 1967, Kennedy 1965), toilet difficulties (De Leon & Mandell 1966, Hundziak et al. 1965, Lovibond 1963), hyperactivity (Patterson et al. 1965), speech defects (Hewett 1965), self-injury (Lovaas et al. 1965, Tate & Baroff 1966), and withdrawal (Allen et al. 1965).

Behavior therapy employed consistently for long periods in a hygienic milieu—as in foster residences for young offenders—may be successful. A limitation of behavior modification, in the context of our interest in criminal careers, is that, after treatment, delinquents and convicts are beyond the therapist's control of reinforcers. Back "on the street," old schedules of reinforcement come into play and a procedure that can correct a habit, like enuresis, may be impotent against the criminogenic reinforcers operating in the actor's environment.

"Success" in behavior modification depends on how a program is administered and on what the program is compared with. Success is a relative term, and how much good "token economies" produce depends on variable criteria. The caution here is not to promise too much, as McConnell (1970) does when he writes:

> I believe that the day has come when we can combine sensory deprivation with drugs, hypnosis, and astute manipulation of reward and punishment to gain almost absolute control over an individual's behavior. . . . We should reshape our society so that we all would be trained from birth to want to do what society wants us to do. We have the techniques now to do it. . . . I foresee the day when we could convert the worst criminal into a decent respectable citizen in the matter of a few months—or perhaps even less time than that (p. 4).

Freedom-lovers would not want McConnell's society even if he and his colleagues could produce it.

Other Cures

The psychotherapies and behavior therapy constitute major efforts to change people. There are, of course, additional procedures.

For example, "milieu therapy" is a grand phrase for getting people out of miserable circumstances and into better ones. "Somatotherapy" and "chemotherapy" attempt to change behaviors by changing physiologies. The inventory of such reformation includes weight reduction, cosmetic surgery, hormone "balancing," shock treatment (chemical or electrical), brain surgery, and the use of mood-altering agents. Chemotherapy helps many people for as long as they "take their pills." Forecasters believe that non-narcotic chemicals will be increasingly acceptable as means of controlling undesirable feelings and actions (Gordon & Helmer 1964).

MEASURING RESULTS

Much scholarly energy has been expended in evaluating efforts to change people. Investigators agree on the canons of scientific evaluation, but they disagree about what one ought to conclude from present research, given the defects of much of it. Recognizing these defects necessitates a statement of scientific research requirements. Logan (1972) lists the following requisites:

1. A program for reforming people must include a clear statement of the *technique* it is using.

Without such specification, it is impossible to tell *what* worked, if anything did.

2. The procedure for changing people must be "capable of routinization."

> This does not mean that it has to be a purely mechanical activity, but it must be something that can be repeated in all its components at different times, with different subjects, by different administrators of the tech-

nique. Thus the technique must not be dependent on any unique personal characteristics of either the original administrator or the original subjects (pp. 378-379).

3. Investigators must be able to divide the offenders to be corrected into treatment (experimental) and control groups. The preferred mode of division is through random assignment.

> The basis of selection for treatment or nontreatment should ideally be a matter of chance, but if subjects are chosen for treatment on some special criteria—such as "amenability," I.Q., or dangerousness—the control group should also be selected on the basis of these same criteria (p. 379).

It is preferable if neither program administrators or other "interested parties" (e.g., judges) partitions the subjects into control and experimental groups.

4. Investigators must be able to show "that the treatment group is in fact receiving treatment as defined, but that the control group is not" (p. 379).

5. "There should be some 'before-and-after' measurement of the behavior that is . . . to be changed, and a comparison made between the two measures. This measurement must be made for both the treatment and control groups" (p. 379).

6. "Success" and "failure" must be clearly defined in advance of intervention. This definition should allow application of measures that are reliable and valid. Therapists' judgments of their efforts and clients' expressions of satisfaction do *not* constitute valid measures of behavior change. Parent's reports of the changed conduct of their children also do *not* constitute valid measures of behavioral change.

Many studies show that it is relatively easy to change verbal behavior, but more difficult to change the actions that the words are supposed to indicate. Thus, parents who participate in behavior modification programs frequently *say* that their children have changed where observers find no such change (Atkeson & Forehand 1978, Eyberg & Johnson 1974, Patterson et al. 1973).

Logan agrees that:

> Success should refer to the correction or prevention of criminal behavior, not to personal adjustment, happiness, mental health, employment, or family relations (p. 379).

7. The criterion of "success" should be employed again after offenders have been "on the streets" for some time. This measurement should apply to both experimental and control subjects, and it should be applied after they are free of supervision.

RESULTS

Logan (1972) read all the books, articles, and government reports in English that he could find that tried to evaluate programs designed to prevent or correct juvenile and adult criminality. His review of 96 such efforts concludes that:

1. "None of these studies of correctional or preventive effectiveness can be described as adequate" (p. 380).

2. "Forty-two of the studies make some attempt at a control group, using that term in the most generous sense and including groups that should more properly be considered comparison groups, rather than controls" (p. 380).

3. Only nine studies tested the effectiveness of a well-defined technique or program.

4. Only three studies satisfied the two criteria of having a proper control group *and* specifying a clear technique.

5. Only *one* study available to Logan at the time of his review employed a proper control group, a clear procedure, and a measurable definition of "success."

However, this lone study did not fulfill the requirement of adequate follow-up in the community.

Replication and Response

Logan's criticism of research inadequacies remains valid. It is the same kind of criticism levelled against evaluation of reformative efforts in general, whether or not the activity to be changed is criminal (Rachman & Wilson 1980).

A few years after Logan's report, a more extensive survey by Lipton, Martinson, and Wilks (1975) also noted deficiencies in tests of correctional efficacy. This survey, and later ones by Fishman (1977) and by Sechrest et al. (1979), confirm the sad conclusion that researchers in criminology do not know "what works."

This conclusion has stimulated a host of replies, most of which avoid the issue of research deficiencies. The replies express alarm that, if we admit that we do not know how to correct offenders efficiently or how to prevent their development, then governments will cease to fund therapeutic efforts and revert to punishing criminals rather than helping them. Replies also suggest that improvement in reformative efforts may be made by (a) better selection of targets (kinds of people to be changed); (b) better selection of techniques tailored to kinds of people and informed by theory; and (c) improved evaluation of these techniques through systematic scanning of program effects (Palmer 1978).

Such prescriptions sound hopeful, but, in response to them, Sechrest and his panel on rehabilitative techniques (1979) remind us that:

> All classification for the purpose of maximizing response to treatment involves a predictive enterprise: the classification is a prediction that the person classified will respond better to one treatment than another. If classification is to be genuinely useful, the accuracy of the prediction must be high. Unfortunately, the history of prediction of human behavior by such means as are usually employed in classification—psychological tests, interviews, and biographical data—affords no grounds for optimism about the approach. The best predictions that have been made are in the area of academic performance, where, after a half century of effort, the correlations achieved are typically only around .50. . . . The success of predictions involving nonintellectual aspects of personality functioning are invariably lower, and correlations of about .35 are considered evidence of success. . . . While correlations of .35, or even lower, can be useful in situations in which a few persons have to be selected from a large population and when the costs of errors are large, this is not the situation that exists in most correctional institutions or organizations (p. 51).

Ross and Gendreau (1980) provide yet another reply to the charge that "nothing works." Their collection of reports of effective corrections shows that some efforts work. The Ross-Gendreau inventory of research is impressive and their thesis is plausible: If one *learns* to be criminal, then one can learn other lessons.

However, we have seen (Volume One, Chapter 6) that "learning" is not one kind of activity and that, whatever it is, it is difficult to define. Ross and Gendreau recognize this and they comment that:

> Behavioral scientists who, for decades, have studied human learning in well controlled laboratory settings are still very much divided as to whether different kinds of learning actually exist, and whether there is a distinction between learning and performance. We do not yet have an adequate theory that can explain how individuals learn even in very well defined controlled situations. There does not even appear to be an exact, comprehensive learning theory for simpler organisms, let alone the human species (p. 5).

The thesis that psychologists can train offenders into lawful styles of life becomes a feasible working assumption *if* trainers can control enough of the learning contingencies long enough. Unfortunately, the "enough's" in this statement remain vague. Surveys of correctional research suggest that re-training offenders works best with minor delinquencies; it works least with major devotions to crime.

Out of the heated debate and the mixture of research, the question posed for dispassionate inquirers is what reasonably to conclude. Any answer must be provisional.

SOME TENTATIVE CONCLUSIONS

1. All therapies help someone, some do nothing but take time, and some therapies make people worse than they were. No balance sheet has been drawn.

2. There is no *science* of corrections.

To have a science would mean that we had empirical warrant for saying that program-X will produce changes of the nature-Y in particular kinds of people-Z with such-and-such frequency.

3. It does not matter how much reformation is produced by correctional efforts *if* responding to crime with treatment has no worse effect than responding to crime with punishment *and if* a correctional response is deemed to be just.

3a. Many delinquents are reared in environments that are obviously damaging. Removing them early, and rearing them in surrogate homes, is no more costly than jailing them.

3b. In response to minor delinquencies—truancy, petty theft, "incorrigibility"—counselling seems more effective than doing nothing or assigning a youth to paper-shuffling probation. Counselling can be made more intensive by employing para-professionals.

3c. "Hard cases" defeat therapies.

Difficult cases arise in which the offender, particularly the youthful offender, commits such a serious crime, or repeated crimes, that a citizenry's sense of justice may not permit treatment. Examples:

Rape

A 14-year-old boy in league with two companions raped a 12-year-old girl—planfully and after a previous failed effort.

Psychological examination of the culprit revealed no mental aberration. His family was intact and sound and he had no prior record of criminal activity. As best we could discern, his crime was produced by an unusual biological development which he enjoyed displaying to his peers. They, in turn, challenged the boy to use his "weapon" rather than merely to show it off, and a rape with witnesses was planned.

The town was aroused by this crime and the local newspaper kept interest alive. Psychologists recommended some threat therapy and shipping the boy to his grandparents 2,000 miles away. This recommendation was *opposed* by a prominent psychiatrist—one of the founders, incidentally, of a major mode of therapy employed in corrections! This psychiatrist, like the community he represented, wanted the boy severely punished.

The judge compromised and sent the boy for a three-month "observational" period in a mental hospital after which he was placed on probation with his grandparents.

The point of this story is that communities, judges, and some therapists have to have their sense of justice appeased, and this may run counter to correctional sense.

Wounding

A 15-year-old boy, in company with a younger buddy, robbed a corner quick-food stand of $70. The boy then held his revolver to the proprietor's head and, despite the victim's pleas, pulled the trigger. The victim is permanently blind.

At the time of this crime, I was attending a conference of criminologists. In informal gatherings at lunch and dinner, I asked my confreres what they would recommend in response to this offense.

A normal response described the law.

My reply was, "Forget the law. Suppose you could do anything you wanted. What, if anything, should be done about this crime?"

I received no reply. Hard cases test justice.

CONCLUSION

Criminal justice systems are not "systems" so much as they are chains of responses that have evolved out of conflicting interests. Some of these interests are vested in political positions and in jobs, and these interests prefer doing more of the same. The next chapter suggests some changes.

7 PRESCRIPTIONS

Abstract • Many students of social affairs work in the spirit of The Enlightenment. They assume that a science of social relations is possible and that it will inform public policy. ○ Doubt challenges hope of a social *science.* ○ Policies express preferences. They therefore can be informed by facts, but not determined by facts alone. • Some recommendations are offered, with recognition that prescriptions represent preferences. Recommendations are: ○ Stop promising "solutions" to the "crime problem." [Nomination of "root causes" of crime is selective. Some "roots of crime" represent values in contemporary societies.] ○ Harden targets. ○ Clarify the concept of "juvenile delinquency." ○ Reduce policing of vice. ○ Stop jailing misdemeanants. ○ Stop involuntary therapy. ○ Reduce use of present prisons. • Social policies that are less than rational flow from mixed moral motives and differential hierarchies of preferences. • Hypocrisy is a normal response to moral conflict. It serves as a social lubricant and personal integrant. It will therefore persist, as will crime.

MANY STUDENTS OF SOCIAL AFFAIRS work in the spirit of The Enlightenment. They trust that their efforts will become scientific, which means that they will develop knowledge from a base of facts. Knowledge is distinguished from mere information in that knowledge ties facts together with clear assumptions to form theories, and these, in turn, are tested for utility by their *differential predictive powers.*

Our excursion through some criminal careers and their attempted explanations casts doubt on the hope that the social studies will become sciences like physics or chemistry. Moreover, what little science of social relations has developed is limited in its ability to guide policy. The entanglement of preferences with interpretations of information means that policies can never be simply deduced from facts. Every policy prescription is tinctured with moral evaluation, and moral preferences, to repeat, are not empirical propositions. They are seldom determined by their empirical consequences or changed by them. Moral assessments are, therefore, disputed, but the disputes are not resolved by any test of "validity."

To prescribe policy is to represent preferences. A catalog of recommendations may be somewhat informed by data, but it nevertheless remains infused with moral judgment.

The recommendations to follow are, then, only suggestions for discussion. They are given without the delusion that one person's preferences are another's or that social choice will be made more rational as it aggregates the votes of many citizens.

1. Stop Promising "Solutions" to the "Crime Problem"

Much recent writing about crime makes promises that cannot be kept. The more popular of these promises suggests that specific, powerful, and manipulable "causes of crime" may be found through more diligent investigation. Or these promises claim that we already know the "root causes" of crime which, when remedied with or without revolution, will reduce criminal activity.

A large inspirational literature proposes that crime is "rooted in social injustice" where "social injustice" is recognized in "poverty," "inequality," "disorderly families," and the lack of "opportunities" for "meaningful work" and "relevant education" (Bazelon 1978, Darrow 1902, Hamparian et al. 1978, Menninger 1978, Sagarin & Karmen 1978, Silberman 1978, Simon 1978, Sommer 1976, pp. 184–185).

Few oppose remedy of these undesirable conditions as an objective that is self-justified. What is at issue is definition, implementation, and the causal relationship between these conditions and crime. Proposals to extirpate such alleged roots of crime suffer from at least six defects:

1. The key concepts are vague. It is impossible to determine where "poverty," "opportunity," "good jobs," and "good education" begin and end *as causes.* Some of the "good jobs" and the "good education" that appear to be available are rejected by some miscreants.

2. Behind any set of nominated "root causes" lie other possible "root causes." There is no end to the possibility of regress in search of sources.

3. We are not certain that anyone's nominated causes are actual causes and, what is more important, we have no knowledge of the crime-causing *powers* of any set of alleged "root causes."

4. The relative powers of any set of nominated causes probably change as the entire social system moves.

5. The usual set of nominated "root causes" omits desirable conditions that may contribute to crime-production. One of these conditions is freedom.

6. Within the framework of freedom, no one knows how to reduce any of the alleged "root causes" at acceptable cost—however these causes are defined and however powerful or weak they may be

as sources of crime. There is no more science of "community development" than there is of "corrections."

The issue is one of conflicting interpretations of history. One interpretation holds that better worlds are, or can be, legislated; the other, that better worlds more frequently evolve. Many journalists and moralists assume the first interpretation; biologists assume the second. If, says one theologian, most of us were to *imagine* an ideal social order—one in which people were more friendly, cooperative, and physically comfortable—then "we could rebuild social structure and economic systems quite easily" (Baum 1980).

To the contrary, neither this moralist nor any social scientist knows how to "rebuild social structures and economic systems" according to plan. Nor does anyone know how to rid the world of "insignificant jobs." Nor does it follow that better housing and better schools make better people; there is good reason to believe that the causal arrow points in the opposite direction. Nor does anyone know how to reduce economic inequality without using force and without endangering the productive capacity of a social system.

Giving people wealth does not produce the same effects as *allowing* them to make it, and the *cultural* consequences of unearned income are not to be confused with the cultural correlates of productivity. Equalizing incomes by placing people "on the dole" ("welfare") does not have the same effect as an equalization of income that has evolved and that is found only among culturally homogeneous populations. Consider the conditions of a relatively crime-free, actual society, Iceland:

> Iceland has no heavy industry. A nation of farmers since its founding, the end of the last century saw Iceland change to a nation of fishermen. The country has no resources of minerals, chemicals, timber, any of the raw products on which an industrial economy must be based. So the industrial revolution passed her by. Having no industry, Iceland has no overconcentration of population, no slums, no unemployment, no mine-blighted areas, no crime (there is less than one murder a year) and . . . no classes. The population is singularly homogeneous. Immigration has been almost unknown since the founding, and few Icelanders emigrate. They all know the names and histories of one another's ancestors. . . . The telephone directories are alphabetically listed by first names, as there are no family names. Every man bears his given name and the name of his father, as does every woman. A married woman does not change her name; throughout her life she is the daugher of her father, not the wife of her husband. . . . Their history . . . is very much alive to them.

> Generally, they are a contented lot. . . . Most of them are, if not rich, comfortable. Competition is not fierce, pressures are low, no one worries much about anything. There are no army, no navy and no air force, so they have never suffered the sorrows of war[1] . . . [They are] a sunny, relaxed people . . . remarkably sophisticated, and as well educated as any people in the world. Literacy is 100 percent. In order to graduate from school, which he must in order to get a job, every Icelander has to speak two languages besides Icelandic. . . . The result is that they are well versed in the literature, arts, history, and politics of the world outside.
>
> Happily it remains the world outside (Sherman 1972).

The world outside cannot be converted into Icelands. There are too many people, for one thing, and they are too diverse culturally. Iceland has population of some 200,000 inhabitants. Their way of living together has developed over 1,000 years.

Cultures evolve; they are not enacted. They develop without plan, not according to design.

This comment on criminogenic conditions indicates that the prescription to protect society by reducing the "root causes" of crime is ideologically selective. Such a recommendation selects causes for their ethicopolitical comfort rather than by their objective connection with crime. Descriptions of idyllic Iceland, for example, and of other relatively crime-free lands like Japan and Norway, tell us that among the roots of crime are cultural diversity, mobility, and freedom from primary group control. Few advocates recommend removing these causes.

2. Harden Targets

Among the first political responses to crime are suggestions to eradicate causes and to deter present and future offenders. But, while political debate ensues, citizens move to make crime more difficult, that is, "to harden targets."

Target-hardening occurs automatically. It is also increased by instruction and with the realization that there is a limit to police protection. Victims and potential victims learn to be wary, although the relationship between actual risk of victimization and wariness varies, as we should expect, with personalities.

---

[1] Scherman here commits the fallacy of *hysteron proteron*. This is the error of "inverting the natural order of reason."

Icelanders have been free of war not because they had no military force. Rather, they had no military force because they were never threatened by war. They were not threatened by war, in turn, because they had no neighbors who wanted what they had.

Personal defense against crime may be as inexpensive as locking one's car or as expensive as installing burglar alarms and barricades. Every preventive action exacts its price and part of the price of responding to crime is a lowering of what is considered to be "the quality of life." Thus, houses in America north of the Rio Grande have long had a different character from domiciles in Latin America. The former are "open-faced," sitting near the center of a plot of land, unguarded, with windows that allow outsiders to peer in from the street. By contrast, Latin houses "turn their backs" to streets. They sit behind walls with few openings, and their windows and terraces turn inward to a guarded and private zone.

The difference has been gradually diminishing with increasing levels of North American crime. We now see the development of entire communities protected by fences, patrols, and alarms. In the last decade classes in self-defense have become increasingly popular. Sales of guns and registrations at shooting ranges have risen as has the use of human and animal guards (Gindick 1981). Twenty-four-hour safe-depositories are increasingly used by businesses and wealthy individuals (Buss 1981).

Common predation—burglary and robbery—changes a way of life. The change is costly, financially and psychologically. Citizens resent this reduction in their standard of living and they are not placated by statistics showing that "You can steal more with a pen than you can with a gun." First concern is with immediate threat, not with long-distance "social harm."

The sense of justice that arises from elevated anxiety about crime calls for isolation of those offenders who are caught. This demand for justice is not diminished by research findings on incarceration or deterrent effects. Citizens react to crime self-defensively, but they also wish their system of justice to do justice as they conceive it.

3. Clarify the Concept of "Juvenile Delinquency"

Western governments have muddled concern for the welfare of youth as they respond to adolescent criminality. Law reform commissions in several jurisdictions (Solicitor General, Canada, 1975) have proposed that so-called "status offenses," such as truancy and "sexual immorality," be removed from the process by which we attend to youthful criminality. Governments have been slow to adopt such reform.

Rationality is constricted here by our ethically motivated wish to be more lenient with "less responsible" youth than with adults "who should know better." However, the *risk of recidivism* is greatest among young offenders and the risk increases with the frequency and violence of the "juvenile's" crimes (Boland & Wilson 1978, Collins 1977, Fishman 1977, Petersilia & Greenwood 1977, Petersilia & Lavin 1978). Petersilia and Lavin conclude that:

> Among those who pursue a continuing career of crime, the onset of serious criminality occurs at approximately 14 years of age. Criminality then peaks in the early 20's, tends to decline until the early 30's, and finally drops sharply in a "maturing out" process. It has been observed that the age group of 14 to 21 years is characterized by a rate of 20 to 40 serious crimes per year; and of 26 to 30 years, about seven. Although there are differences among offense types in this dependence between age and commission rate, an early peak followed by a steady decline is typical.

If societal protection were the major objective of policy, young felons—particularly the violent ones—would be restrained rather than placed on probation. "Restraint" here includes having costs added to crimes. Costs can be flexible, but they must be punitive in the sense that punishment expresses to offenders disapproval of their conduct and the promise of additional costs if criminal careers are continued.

4. Reduce Policing of Vice

Vice in private places should not be policed at all. Surveillance is too expensive.

Criminal codes need a pruning of their rosters of "sex crimes." The citizenry will probably agree that the following kinds of sometime-crimes can be safely ignored: Fornication and cohabitation, homosexuality, sodomy, and bestiality. Bigamy and transvestism can also be ignored unless damaging fraud is involved.

The citizenry may not yet be ready to follow suggestions, such as Morris, Hawkins (1970), and others have advanced, that abortion, incest, statutory rape, and pornography be decriminalized. It is possible, though, that many jurisdictions are prepared to narrow definitions of incest and of statutory rape. In fact, thirteen of the American states no longer have laws against statutory rape.

The contest about induced abortion is tangled. It is in part a matter of who pays for the surgery, where government subsidy is proposed and where some citizens object to their taxes funding what they regard as an immoral operation. However, regardless of subsidy, the conflict remains a moral one concerning the rightness of intentionally ending embryonic life. And moral quarrels are seldom, if ever, resolved by applying reason to facts.

Citizens may still wish to prohibit what they consider to be offensive public displays such as obscene exhibitions or whores' street solicitation. However, surveillance of massage parlors and bawdy houses is costly compared with its mild benefits, and some jurisdictions may now be ready to license whorehouses as they are in West Germany and parts of Nevada.

Reduced attention to vice should be extended to "narcotics control" acts as these are worded in many countries. The schedule of so-called "narcotics"[2] needs revision to bring it into line with public morality and our knowledge of the differentially damaging effects of the many "comforting chemicals."

For example, it is inconsistent to penalize the production, sale, and use of marijuana and cocaine on the ground that they are damaging, physically or psychologically, while permitting distribution of the common intoxicant, ethyl alcohol, and the deadly weed, tobacco. By contrast with our legally permitted anesthetics and stimulants, even the opiates are relatively innocent in their effect on *physical* health. What they contribute to a person's psychic well-being is another issue, but it is an issue that can as legitimately be raised about "demon rum."

Impaired driving can still be proscribed, of course, but it need be no government's business whether a person carries a pack of cigarettes or a pack of "reefers."

This is no prescription for "legalization" in the sense of licensing, and hence tacitly approving, use of marijuana and cocaine. It is a prescription for ignoring these products.

The opiates are another matter. The habitual use of opiates has debilitating psychological and moral effects. These agents take people "out of this world." There is, of course, a thesis that technology increasingly makes more people useless (Piel 1961) and that, as in

---

[2] To narcotize is to induce a state of drowsiness. A narcotic is a depressant. It is an agent that produces numbness, stupor, and, in sufficient dosage, coma and death. Euphoria is experienced along the way.

Many natural and synthetic chemicals forbidden under "narcotics acts" are not depressants. Some are stimulants, like cocaine, and some are best described as psychotropic agents, meaning that their principal effect is "mind-turning." *Cannabis sativa* is the most popular and ancient of these mood-altering agents, but human beings have ingested a vast pharmacy of chemicals to change their feelings about themselves and their worlds.

There is good reason, then, to refer to the collection of depressants, stimulants, and other mood-changers not as "drugs," since not all are, but as "comforting chemicals" (Nettler 1976) since they are taken principally for their comforts and not for nutrition or medicine.

Huxley's *Brave New World* (1960), people ought to be able to take a pill—*Soma*—and opt out for a while. However, until that *Brave New World* arrives, the effects of opiate addiction upon work and upon commitment to others are damaging.

Two opposed courses are recommended in response to the lucrative "dope trade." The "liberal" recommendation is to sell opiates through prescription by licensed physicians. Under this policy, accumulation of large quantities of the opiates can be proscribed as evidence of intent to sell and this can be prosecuted as criminal.

A "conservative" argument contends that legalization of the opiates encourages their expanded use while it does not reduce illegal traffic. This argument rests on alleged evidence of increased use with legalization in other countries and on the assumption that legalization removes "the moral inhibitions . . . from things that were previously regarded as forms of 'vice'." (Arkes 1974, p. 45).

Given the enormous profits made in dealing opiates, the conservative prescription requires "warfare" to implement it. That is, normal policing will not control the narcotics industry. Extreme action might. Extreme action includes covert surveillance, use of *agents provocateurs,* and the death penalty for traders in opiates.

On this issue, as with many social policies, we are constrained by competing values so that no one rational outcome is probable.

5. Stop Jailing Misdemeanants

The nuisance crimes like public drunkenness and ordinary brawling can be economically handled by arrest—that is, by stopping the action—followed by issuance of a summons to a hearing if plaintiffs are involved. Without complainants, such common offenses should be ignored.

Detoxification centers are in use and should replace jailhouse "drunk tanks." There is no deterrent or reformative value in sentencing alcoholics to jail. Social services can be offered alcoholics and other sick misdemeanants during their hospitalization, but acceptance of such service should be voluntary.

Goldfarb (1975, 1980) proposes a flexible set of responses to misdemeanors that deserves exploration as a means of reducing incarceration. Among his suggestions is the end of money bail to secure appearance of the accused. This suggestion achieves fairness among defendants with different resources. It is resisted, however, because Goldfarb, like others, recognizes the need to detain dangerous persons. Preventive detention without the right to bail offends civil libertarians (Nagel 1980, p. 213) who believe that abuses of bail are less important than the possible abuse of holding procedures. Once again, morality intrudes upon efficiency.

6. Stop Involuntary Therapy

The poor record of people-changing and the immorality of coerced behavioral modification cannot justify using prisons for corrections. Educational and therapeutic services can always be offered, but these offerings are most effective when they are voluntarily elected and least effective when they are coerced (Cross 1971).

This recommendation is not concerned with the "therapy" of removing juveniles from damaging environments. It is addressed, rather, to the use of an adult sentence as an instrument of correction and it runs counter to a major assumption of indeterminate sentencing. The indeterminate sentence has developed on the assumptions that correctional devices are known and that experts can tell when criminals have been cured. Apropos these assumptions, the American Psychological Association's Board of Social and Ethical Responsibility for Psychology recently established a 12-person task force to assess the role of psychologists in criminal justice systems. The task force questioned all American psychologists (N = 349) whose primary employment was an agency of criminal or juvenile justice, and Monahan (1980) edited the final report.

This report shows that the overwhelming majority (83.7%) of these psychologists believe that indeterminate sentencing should either be modified or eliminated. The responding psychologists justify their opinions by referring to:

a. the inadequacy of treatment and assessment methods,
b. the lack of clarity in release criteria,
c. institutional abuses of procedures, and
d. the contamination of client-treatment-agent relationships by conflicting organizational goals (p. 131).

Whether or not indeterminate sentencing is modified or abandoned, a majority of these psychologists (75.8%) approve of custodial efforts at behavior modification. However, these respondents recognize possibilities of abuse and a majority recommend that treatment of whatever sort, be an *opportunity* rather than a *right* or a *requirement* (p. 139). They make an exception for "dangerous" felons. In such cases most psychologists approve of enforced medication to pacify the violent, but they disapprove of coerced psychotherapy, shock treatment, or psychosurgery (p. 141).

It would be interesting to extend the APA survey to the citizenry to ascertain who approves or disapproves of surgical intervention, as in the dilemma faced by Judge O'Brien in the case of the persistent rapist (p. 63). It is noted that decisions such as O'Brien's *force* other people to pay for his ethics.

Another moral dilemma concerns forcing schooling upon inmates. The former warden, George Beto (1980), believes that schooling should be compulsory for uneducated inmates since, in the Texas prisons he administered, 96 percent of the convicts were school dropouts with an average IQ of 80. About one-fifth of these inmates were illiterate and the average reading ability of the total population was that of a normal fifth-grader. It remains a tough question whether compulsory schooling works for post-adolescents with low IQs. However, if prison populations were reduced and sentences shortened, as recommended below, schooling could be provided "on the outside" for those who want it.

7. Reduce Use of Present Prisons

Many voices have urged that present prisons be abandoned (Mitford 1974, Rector 1977, Sommer 1976). Condemnation of prison decries the "warehousing" of large numbers of thieves and brawlers behind walls where they have years in which to get to know one another, to exchange criminal skills, and to infect one another with their varieties of distemper.

We pay an enormous price for such incarceration, and one that is beyond full calculation. Current practice herds together an assortment of bad actors and forces them to eat, sleep, play, and work with one another. What occurs, over and over, is that bad action becomes preferred action, and the worst actors rule. They teach one another that the world is a jungle and that one should deceive outsiders, defend one's "brothers," and rape, steal, and kill in accordance with inmates' "justice."

For some wrong guys who become defined as "right guys," prison is fun. For others prison is no more unpleasant than daily life on the street. In prison, these incompetents continue to fight, fornicate, and brutalize. A response to crime that produces this activity is irrational.

Options

However unpleasant they are, present prisons will not be closed until viable options are invented to replace them. Commonly suggested diversions from prison include increased use of sentences of fine, restitution, orders to provide "social service," and remand to "community correctional facilities." However, these substitutes have limited application and they will not satisfy some of the realistic objectives of the criminal law.

We have seen the limitations of restitution (Chapter 1), including the fact that it runs into the difficulty that a majority of inmates have poor money-earning skills (Hickey & Scharf 1980). Adequate restitution would require more time and earnings than many can accommodate and a threat of detention will have to be held over welchers on restitution contracts.

Furthermore, fine, restitution, and service orders will not isolate persistently offensive persons. Such sentences may not add a sufficient cost to crime to deter potential bad actors, and they may not always do justice.

Decarceration advocates like to point out that something like 90 percent of inmates could be released "without danger" to society. However, this statement does not tell us which kind of danger, and how much of it, is thus obviated. It does not include the psychological, as well as financial, "danger" that ordinary street-crime and burglary produce. This is the sense of "danger" that changes the quality of life, as mentioned earlier. In addition, such a statement about the innocuous nature of most prisoners does not assess the "danger" of decreased deterrence with less painful responses to crime. In short, assurances about the mildness of the majority of inmates encounters all the deficiencies of our predictive devices.

Advocates of decarceration will make a stronger case as they are able to specify *what* should be done in response to criminal activity. It is not enough to say, "Don't put them in prison," until some better—more just and more effective—responses have been invented. We look, then for options.

Space permits mention of some suggested responses, but not their full description. For example, it has been proposed that victims of violent crimes sue their assailants for damages under tort law (Burden 1978, Cross 1971, p. 392). This suggestion encounters the same difficulty as restitution.

It is increasingly proposed that chronic rapists, wounding brawlers, and certain classes of killer, like mass murderers, professional "hit men," and "idealistic" assassins, either be consigned to small, self-sustaining quarantine stations in remote areas (Solicitor General, Alberta, 1978) or, in the case of the killers, be executed (Berns 1979, Sterling 1978).

Other suggestions call for redesign of jails. For example, Goldfarb (1980) believes that detention facilities should be built with three wings. Wing One would be used for pretrial detention of dangerous offenders. It would have no cells. Wing Two, segregated from other parts of the facility, would be used for classification and referral, a function that is to be completed within 48 hours. It would be particularly useful in attending to children in trouble with the law, but violent youngsters would be isolated in Wing One.

Wing Three would consist of dormitories for inmates in community corrections programs—for those on work release, in halfway houses, on restitution contracts, and those serving part-time prison sentences.

In addition to these suggestions, some "futurologists" consider that, by the year 2000, prisons that are required to add a cost to crime will be clearly punitive. However, the punishment for most felons will be short, sharp, and hygienic. Detention centers will be completely automated. According to this image, offenders who need the pain of reprobation and arrest will be sentenced to *short terms spent alone.*

Food will be served automatically on aircraft-type trays. Sensory stimulation will be provided by books, earphone radio, and time-controlled television. Inmates can exercise, if they wish, according to Canadian Airforce 5-BX instructions for isolates. No visitors will be permitted other than prison personnel. Counselling will be provided on request. Offenders given this short, sharp "rap" will serve sentences about ten percent the length of those currently mandated.

This vision of the future is intended to destroy the happiness of prison camaraderie and to remove the possibility of prison riot, rape, and moral infection. It also relieves jailers of the necessity of living the lives of inmates.

Objections to short, solo sentences are either moral—inmates should not live alone—or incorrect. Moral objections can be quarreled, but they are seldom satisfied. Incorrect objections decry "sensory deprivation" where none is recommended, other than deprivation of companionship.

However, these and other suggestions of substitutes for present prisons are not likely to be tried because the public doesn't care much what happens to convicts as long as they are isolated and detained. The prison bureaucracy moves slowly, and moralists who deplore present jails find moral reasons for objecting to feasible changes.

CONCLUSION

Given the perennial conflicts between mixed moral motives and efficient means toward collective ends, we cannot conclude that governmental response to crime will soon be marked by increased rationality.

Irrationality increases with conflict, which means that it increases with the diversity of desires within one person or within a collectivity. Arrow's theorem applies. In a heterogeneous society, logically consistent policy may be impossible, and it may be impossible in respect of any public issue from the production of energy and other wealth (Bloom 1953) to the distribution of justice and determination of "the best way" of responding to crime (Firey 1969).

Constancy of Hypocrisy

The normal response to moral conflict is hypocrisy (Warriner 1958). A normal tactic of the hypocritical is to call the old, bad thing a new name, as per Orwellian "Newspeak." Thus as we approach Orwell's *Nineteen Eighty-Four* (1948), it is no surprise to find that ethnic quotas become "goals," censorship becomes "rule-making" (Bennett 1978, 1979), punishment becomes "rehabilitation," and prisons become "correctional institutions."

Between ourselves, hypocrisy allows us to get along when we disagree. Within one's self, hypocrisy preserves sanity when the individual is torn between doing something or nothing, the right thing and the practical thing.

Hypocrisy is a social lubricant and a personal integrant. It will persist, as will crime.

REFERENCES

Allen, K.E. et al. 1965. "Effects of social reinforcement on isolate behavior of a nursery school child." In L.P. Ullmann & L. Krasner (eds.), *Case Studies in Behavior Modification.* New York: Holt, Rinehart, Winston.

Allport, F.H. 1939. "Rule and custom as individual variation of behavior distributed upon a continuum of conformity." *Amer.Jour.Sociol.,* 44:897–921.

Alpert, R. 1972. "A fever of ethnicity." *Commentary,* 53:68–73.

American Psychiatric Association. 1974. *Clinical Aspects of the Violent Individual.* Washington, D.C.: The Association.

American Psychological Association. 1980. "Brief of American Psychological Association as amicus curiae." *Amer.Psych.,* 35:1028–1043.

Andenaes, J. 1952. "General prevention: Illusion or reality?" *Jour.Crim.Law, Criminol., & Police Sci.,* 43:176–198.

Andenaes, J. 1966. "The general preventive effects of punishment." *Univ.Penn.Law Rev.,* 114:949–983.

——. 1974. *Punishment and Deterrence.* Ann Arbor: Univ. Mich. Press.

Appelbaum, S. 1977. *The Anatomy of Change: The Menninger Foundation Report on Testing the Effects of Psychotherapy.* New York: Plenum.

Arendt, H. 1964. *Eichmann in Jerusalem: A Report on the Banality of Evil.* New York: Viking.

Argyris, C. 1964. "T-groups for organizational effectiveness." *Harvard Bus.Rev.,* 42:60–74.

Arkes, H. 1974. "The problem of Kenneth Clark." *Commentary,* 58:37–46.

Arrow, K.J. 1974. *The Limits of Organization.* New York: Norton.

——. 1978. *Social Choice and Individual Values.* 2nd ed., New Haven: Yale U.P.

Atkeson, B.M. & R. Forehand. 1978. "Parent behavioral training for problem children." *Jour.Ab.Child Psych.,* 6:449–460.

Bailey, W.C. 1977. "Imprisonment v. the death penalty as a deterrent to murder." *Law & Beh.,* 1:239–260.
——. 1980. "Deterrence and the celerity of the death penalty: A neglected question in deterrence research." *Soc.Forces,* 58:1308–1333.
Bailey, W.C. and R.P. Lott. 1976. "Crime, punishment, and personality: An examination of the deterrence question." *Jour.Crim.Law & Crim.,* 67:49–109.
Bard, M. & D. Sangrey. 1979. *The Crime Victim's Book.* New York: Basic Books.
Bar-Hillel, M. 1978. "The base-rate fallacy in probability judgments." In press, *Acta Psychologica.*
Barnett, C. 1965. *The Swordbearers: Supreme Command in the First World War.* New York: Signet.
Baum, G. 1980. Interview with E. Morris. *Homemaker's Magazine,* 15:58–76.
Bazelon, D.L. 1969. *Cross v. Harris.* Washington, D.C., Circuit Court of Appeals, 418:1095–1110.
——. 1978. "The hidden politics of American criminology." *Fed.Prob.,* 32:3–9.
Becker, G.S. 1971. *The Economics of Discrimination.* Chicago: Univ. Chicago Press.
Benn, S.I. 1967. "State." In P. Edwards (ed.), *The Encyclopedia of Philosophy.* New York: Macmillan.
Bennett, J.V. 1964. "The sentence: Its relation to crime and rehabilitation." In *Of Prisons and Justice.* Senate Document #70, 88th Congress. Washington, D.C.: U.S. GPO.
Bennett, W.J. 1978. "Censorship for the common good." *Pub.Int.,* #52:98–102.
——. 1979. "Communications: Censorship for the common good." *Pub.Int.* #54:115–117.
Bequai, A. 1978. *Computer Crime.* Toronto: Heath.
Bergin, A.E. 1971. "The evaluation of therapeutic outcomes." In S.L. Garfield & A.E. Bergin (eds.), *Handbook of Psychotherapy and Behavior Change: An Empirical Analysis.* New York: Wiley.
Berk, R.A. et al. 1977. *A Measure of Justice: An Empirical Study of Changes in the California Penal Code, 1955–1971.* New York: Academic Press.
Berkson, J. 1955. "Smoking and lung cancer, some observations on two recent reports." *Jour.Amer.Stat.Assoc.,* 53:28.

Berne, E. 1964. *Games People Play: The Psychology of Human Relationships.* New York: Grove.

Berns, W. 1979. *For Capital Punishment: Crime and the Morality of the Death Penalty.* New York: Basic Books.

Bernstein, I.N. et al. 1977. "Societal reaction to deviants: The case of criminal defendants." *Amer.Sociol.Rev.,* 42:743–755.

Beto, G. 1980. "Commentary." In C.H. Foust & D.R. Webster (eds.), *An Anatomy of Criminal Justice.* Lexington, Mass.: Lexington Books.

Black, D. 1976. *The Behavior of Law.* New York: Academic Press.

Blau, P.M. 1964. *Exchange and Power in Social Life.* New York: Wiley.

Bloom, C.C. 1953. "Is a consistent governmental economic policy possible?". In A.D. Ward (ed.), *Goals of Economic Life.* New York: Harper.

Bloom, L. & R. Riemer. 1949. *Removal and Return: The Socio-Economic Effects of the War on Japanese Americans.* Los Angeles: Univ. Calif. Press.

Blum, D.J. 1980. "Trials and errors: Jury system is found guilty of shortcomings in complex cases." *Wall St.Jour.,* 102:1, 16 (June 9).

Blumstein, A. & J. Cohen. 1973. "A theory of the stability of punishment." *Jour.Crim.Law & Crim.,* 64:198–207.

Blumstein, A. et al. 1977. "The dynamics of a homeostatic punishment process." *Jour.Crim. Law & Crim.,* 67:317–334.

Blumstein, A. et al. (eds.), 1978. *Deterrence and Incapacitation: Estimating the Effects of Criminal Sanctions on Crime Rates.* Washington, D.C.: National Academy of Sciences.

Blumstein, A. & S. Moitra. 1979. "An analysis of the time series of the imprisonment rate in the states of the United States: A further test of the stability of punishment hypothesis." *Jour.Crim. Law & Crim.,* 70N376–390.

Boland, B. & J.Q. Wilson. 1978. "Age, crime, and punishment." *Pub.Int.,* #51:22–34.

Bondeson, U. 1975. "A critical survey of correctional treatment studies in Scandinavia, 1945–1974." In E. van den Haag & R. Martinson (eds.), *Crime Deterrence and Offender Career Project.* New York: Office of Economic Opportunity.

Bottomley, A.K. 1979. *Criminology in Focus: Past Trends and Future Prospects.* London: Robertson.

Bowen, D.R. 1965. *The Explanation of Judicial Voting Behavior from Sociological Characteristics of Judges.* Ph.D. dissertation. New Haven: Yale University.

Bowers, W.J. (ed.). 1974. *Executions in America*. Lexington, Mass.: Lexington Books.

Bowers, W.J. and G.L. Pierce. 1980. "Arbitrariness and discrimination under post-*Furman* capital statutes." *Crime & Delinq.*, 26:563–635.

Braucht, G.N. et al. 1980. "Victims of violent death: A critical review." *Psych.Bull*, 87:309–333.

Bremer, J. 1959. *Asexualization: A Follow-up Study of 244 Cases*. New York: Macmillan.

Brewer, C. & J. Lait. 1980. *Can Social Work Survive?* London: Temple Smith.

Brier, S.S. & S.E. Fienberg. 1980. "Recent econometric modelling of crime and punishment: Support for the deterrence hypothesis?" In S.E. Fienberg & A.J. Reiss, Jr., (eds.), *Indicators of Crime and Criminal Justice: Quantitative Studies*. Washington, D.C.: U.S. GPO.

Broader, D.W. 1959. "The University of Chicago jury project." *Nebraska Law Rev.*, 38:744–760.

Bruce, L. 1972. *How to Talk Dirty and Influence People*. Chicago: Playboy Press.

Bullock, H.A. 1961. "Significance of the racial factor in length of prison sentences." *Jour.Crim.Law, Crim., & Police Sci.*, 52:411–417.

Burden, O.P. 1978. "Legal group urges crime victims to sue their assailants." *Law Enforcement News*, 4:5 (Dec. 11).

Burgess, A.W. and L.L. Holmstrom. 1974. "Rape trauma syndrome." *Amer.Jour.Psychiat.*, 131:981–986.

Burlingame, R. 1954. *Henry Ford*. New York: New American Library.

Campbell, J.P. & M.D. Dunnette. 1968. "Effectiveness of T-group experiences in managerial training and development." *Psych.Bull.*, 70:73–114.

Camus, A. 1956. *The Rebel*. New York: Knopf.

Canada, Ministry of Justice. 1965. *Capital Punishment: Material Relating to Its Purpose and Value*. Ottawa: Queen's Printer.

Canadian Press. 1981. "Traditional Islamic law on way back." (Feb. 9).

Carney, L.P. 1980. *Corrections: Treatment and Philosophy*. Englewood Cliffs, N.J.: Prentice-Hall.

Carr-Hill, R.A. & N.H. Stern. 1979. *Crime, the Police, and Criminal Statistics*. New York: Academic Press.

Chalidze, V. 1977. *Criminal Russia: Essays on Crime in the Soviet Union*. Trans. by P.S. Falla. New York: Random House.

Chan, J.B.L. & R.V. Ericson. 1981. *Decarceration and the Economy of Penal Reform*. Toronto: Centre of Criminology, University of Toronto.

Chandler, D.B. 1976. *Capital Punishment in Canada.* Toronto: McClelland & Stewart.

Chandler, D.B. et al. 1976. *Ethnic Bias in Commuting Mandatory Death Sentences, Canada 1946-1962.* Unpublished monograph. Honolulu: Department of Sociology, University of Hawaii-Manoa.

Chapel, J.L. 1967. "Treatment of a case of school phobia by reciprocal inhibition." *Can.Psychiat. Assoc.Jour.,* 12:25–28.

Chiricos, T.G. & G.P. Waldo. 1970. "Punishment and crime: An examination of some empirical evidence." *Soc.Probs.,* 18:200–217.

——. 1975. "Socioeconomic status and criminal sentencing: An empirical assessment of a conflict proposition." *Amer.Sociol.Rev.,* 40:753–772.

Church, G. & C.D. Carnes. 1973. *The Pit.* New York: Outerbridge & Lazard.

Clark, G. 1969. "Black Tuesday in Montreal: What happens when the police strike" *The New York Times Magazine,* p. 45 (Nov. 16).

Clarke, S.H. & G.G. Koch. 1976. "The influence of income and other factors on whether criminal defendants go to prison." *Law & Soc.Rev.,* 11:57–92.

Cocozza, J.J. & H.J. Steadman. 1974. "Some refinements in the measurement and prediction of dangerous behavior." *Amer.Jour. Psychiat.,* 131:1012–1014.

——. 1976. "The failure of psychiatric predictions of dangerousness: Clear and convincing evidence." *Rutgers Law Rev.,* 29:1084–1101.

Cohen, J. 1978. "The incapacitative effect of imprisonment: A critical review of the literature." In A. Blumstein et al. (eds.), *Deterrence and Incapacitation: Estimating the Effects of Criminal Sanctions on Crime Rates.* Washington, D.C.: National Academy of Sciences.

Cohen, L.E. & J.R. Kluegel. 1978. "Determinants of juvenile court dispositions." *Amer.Sociol.Rev.,* 43:162–176.

Coleman, J.S. & S.D. Kelly. 1976. "Education." In W. Gorham & N. Glazer (eds.), *The Urban Predicament.* Washington, D.C.: The Urban Institute.

Collingwood, R.G. 1977. *An Essay on Philosophical Method.* Oxford: Oxford U.P.

Collins, J. 1977. *Offender Careers and Restraint: Probabilities and Policy Implications.* Washington, D.C.: Law Enforcement and Assistance Administration.

Committee on Government Operations. 1977. *Staff Study of Computer Security in Federal Programs.* Washington, D.C.: U.S. GPO.

Cook, P.J. 1977. "Punishment and crime: A critique of current findings concerning the preventive effects of punishment." *Law & Contemp.Probs.,* 41:164–204.

———. 1980. "The implications of deterrence and incapacitation research for policy evaluation." In C. Foust & R. Webster (eds.), *An Anatomy of Criminal Justice*. Lexington, Mass.: Heath.

Cousineau, F.D. 1976. *General Deterrence of Crime:* An Analysis. Ph.D. dissertation. Edmonton: Department of Sociology, The University of Alberta.

Cousineau, F.D. & J.E. Veevers. 1972. "Juvenile justice: An analysis of the Canadian Young Offenders' Act." In C. Boydell et al. (eds.), *Deviant Behavior and Societal Reaction*. Toronto: Holt.

Crooks, R.C. 1970. "The effects of an interracial preschool program upon racial preference, knowledge of racial differences, and racial identification." *Jour.Soc.Issues,* 26:137–144.

Cross, A.R.N. 1971. *Punishment, Prison, and the Public: An Assessment of Penal Reform in Twentieth Century England by an Armchair Penologist*. London: Stevens.

Danet, B. et al. 1980. "Threats to the life of the president: An analysis of linguistic issues." *Jour.Media Law & Practice,* 1:180–190.

Dann, R. 1935. *The Deterrent Effect of Capital Punishment*. Bulletin #29. Friends' Social Service Series. Philadelphia: Meeting of Friends.

Darroch, A.G. & W.G. Marston. 1977. "The social class basis of ethnic residential segregation: The Canadian case." *Amer.Jour.Sociol.,* 77:491–510.

Darrow, C.S. 1902. *Crime and Criminals*. Chicago: Kerr.

Davidson, D. 1981. *Essays on Actions and Events*. Oxford: Clarendon.

deLeeuw, F. et al. 1976. "Housing." In W. Gorham & N. Glazer (eds.), *The Urban Predicament*. Washington, D.C.: The Urban Institute.

De Leon, G. & W. Mandell. 1966. "A comparison of conditioning and psychotherapy in the treatment of functional enuresis." *Jour.Clin.Psych.,* 22:326–330.

Donnerstein, E. 1980. "Aggressive erotica and violence against women." *Jour.Person.Soc.Psych.,* 39:269–277.

Dorin, D.D. 1981. "Two different worlds: Criminologists, justices and racial discrimination in the imposition of capital punishment in rape cases." *Journal of Criminal Law & Criminology,* 72:1667–1698.

Duncan, O.D. 1967. "Discrimination against Negroes." *Annals Amer.Aca.Pol.Soc.Scis.,* 371:85–103.

Dworkin, R.H. et al. 1977. "Genetic influences on the organization and development of personality." *Develop.Psych.,* 13:164–165.

Edwards, A.L. 1957. *The Social Desirability Variable in Personality Assessment and Research.* New York: Dryden.

Efran, M.G. 1974. "The effect of physical appearance on the judgment of guilt, interpersonal attraction, and severity of recommended punishment in a simulated jury task." *Jour.Exper.Res.Person.,* 8:45–64.

Ehrlich, I. 1974. "Participation in illegitimate activities: An economic analysis." In G.S. Becker & W.M. Landes (eds.), *Essays in the Economics of Crime and Punishment.* New York: National Bureau of Economic Research.

———. 1975. "The deterrent effect of capital punishment: A question of life and death." *Amer.Econ.Rev.,* 65:397–417.

Ehrlich, I. & R. Mark. 1978. "Deterrence and economics: A perspective on theory and evidence." In J.M. Yinger & S.J. Cutler (eds.), *Major Social Issues: A Multidisciplinary View.* New York: Free Press.

Ellis, A. 1962. *Reason and Emotion in Psychotherapy.* New York: Stuart.

———. 1964. *The Theory and Practice of Rational-Emotive Psychotherapy.* New York: Stuart.

Ellis, E.M. et al. 1981. "An assessment of long-term reaction to rape." *Jour. Ab.Psych.,* 90:263–266.

Elmhorn, K. 1965. "Study in self-reported delinquency among school-children in Stockholm." In K.O. Christiansen (ed.), *Scandinavian Studies in Criminology.* Vol. 1. London: Tavistock.

Ennis, B.J. & T.R. Litwak. 1976. "Psychiatry and the presumption of expertise: Flipping coins in the courtroom." *Calif.Law Rev.,* 62:693–752.

Epstein, S. 1979. "The stability of behavior. I: On predicting most of the people much of the time." *Jour.Person.Soc.Psych.,* 37:1097–1126.

———. 1980. "The stability of behavior. II: Implications for psychological research." *Amer.Psych.,* 35:790–806.

Ervin, F.R. & J.R. Lion. 1969. "Clinical evaluation of the violent patient." In D. Mulvihill & M. Tumin (eds.), *Crimes of Violence: A Staff Report Submitted to the National Commission on the Causes and Prevention of Violence.* Washington, D.C.: U.S. GPO.

Eyberg, S.M. & S.M. Johnson. 1974. "Multiple assessment of behavior modification with families." *Jour.Consult.Clin.Psych.,* 42:594–606.

Farnsworth, P.R. 1937. "Changes in attitudes toward men during college years." *Jour.Soc.Psych.,* 8:274–279.

———. 1949. In R.T. LaPiere & P.R. Farnsworth. *Social Psychology.* 3rd ed. New York: McGraw-Hill.

Fay, B. 1975. *Social Theory and Political Practice.* London: George Allen & Unwin.

Feild, H.S. 1979. "Rape trials and jurors' decisions: A psycholegal analysis of the effects of victim, defendant, and case characteristics." *Law & Hum.Beh.,* 3:261–284.

Feinberg, J. 1970. *Doing and Deserving: Essays in the Theory of Responsibility.* Princeton: Princeton U.P.

Finckenauer, J.O. 1979. "Scared crooked." *Psych.Today,* 13:6.

Finkelstein, M. 1966. "Application of statistical decision theory to jury discrimination cases." *Harvard Law Rev.,* 80:338–376.

Firey, W. 1969. "Limits to economy in crime and punishment." *Soc.Sci.Quart.,* 50:72–77.

Fisher, F.M. & D. Nagin. 1978. "On the feasibility of identifying the crime function in a simultaneous model of crime rates and sanction levels." In A. Blumstein et al. (eds.), *Deterrence and Incapacitation: Estimating the Effects of Criminal Sanctions on Crime Rates.* Washington, D.C.: National Academy of Sciences.

Fishman, R. 1977. *Criminal Recidivism in New York City: An Evaluation of the Impact of Rehabilitation and Diversion Services.* New York: Praeger.

Fleisher, B.M. 1966. *The Economics of Delinquency.* Chicago: Quadrangle Books.

Fly, J.W. & G.R. Reinhart. 1980. "Racial separation during the 1970s: The case of Birmingham." *Soc.Forces,* 58:1255–1262.

Fontaine, G. & R. Kiger. 1978. "The effects of defendant dress and supervision on judgments of simulated jurors: An exploratory study." *Law & Hum.Beh.,* 2:63–71.

Frailey, F.W. 1978. "How Washington winks at corruption in unions." *U.S. News & World Report,* 84:62–64 (Jan. 23).

Fredlund, M.C. 1975. "The economics of animal systems." In G. Tullock (ed.), *Frontiers of Economics.* Blacksburg, Va.: University Publications.

Frey, W.H. 1979. "Central city white flight: Racial and nonracial causes." *Amer.Sociol.Rev.,* 44:425–448.

Friedan, B. 1973. Cited by *Newsweek,* 81:63 (May 14).

Friedman, L.M. 1975. *The Legal System: A Social Science Perspective.* New York: Russell Sage.

Galaway, B. 1977. "The use of restitution." *Crime & Delinq.,* 23:57–67.

———. 1980. "Is restitution practical?" In M.D. Schwartz et al (eds.), *Corrections:* An Issues Approach. Cincinnati: Anderson.

Galen, R.S. & S.R. Gambino. 1975. *Beyond Normality: The Predictive Value and Efficiency of Medical Diagnosis.* New York: Wiley.

Garfinkel, H. 1949. "Research note on inter- and intra-racial homicides." *Soc.Forces,* 27:369–381.

Geerken, M. & W.R. Gove. 1977. "Deterrence, overload, and incapacitation: An empirical evaluation." *Soc.Forces,* 56:424–447.

Gendreau, P. & R.R. Ross. 1980. *Correctional Potency: Treatment and Deterrence on Trial.* Unpublished ms. Burritt's Rapids, Ontario: Rideau Correctional Centre, and Ottawa: University of Ottawa.

Gibbs, J.P. 1966. "Sanctions." *Soc.Probs.,* 14:147–159.

———. 1975. *Crime, Punishment, and Deterrence.* New York: Elsevier.

Gibson, J.L. 1978. "Race as a determinant of criminal sentences: A methodological critique and a case study." *Law & Soc.Rev.,* 12:455–478.

Gindick, T. 1981. "Self-defense in vogue: The wealthy prepare for battle." *Los Angeles Times,* pp. 1, 10–11 (Mar. 26).

Glasser, W. 1965. *Reality Therapy: A New Approach to Psychiatry.* New York: Harper & Row.

Glueck, S. 1936. *Crime and Justice.* Boston: Little, Brown.

Goffman, E. 1963. *Stigma: Notes on the Management of Spoiled Identity.* Englewood Cliffs, N.J.: Prentice-Hall.

Goldfarb, R.L. 1975. *Ransom.* New York: Harper & Row.

———. 1980. "A proposal for jail reform." In C.H. Foust & D.R. Webster (eds.), *An Anatomy of Criminal Justice.* Lexington, Mass.: Lexington Books.

Goldkamp, J.S. 1976. "Minorities as victims of police shootings: Interpretations of racial disproportionality and police use of deadly force." *Justice Sys.Jour.,* 2:169–183.

Goldstein, J.H. & J. Katz. 1960. "Dangerousness and mental illness: Some observations on the decision to release persons acquitted by reason of insanity." *Yale Law Jour.,* 70:225–239.

Gordon, R.A. 1977. "A critique of the evaluation of Patuxent Institution, with particular attention to the issues of dangerousness and recidivism." *Bulletin of the American Academy of Psychiatry and the Law,* 5:210–255.

Gordon, T.J. & O. Helmer. 1964. *Report on a Long-Range Forecasting Study.* Santa Monica: Rand Corp.

Gottfredson, M.R. & D. Gottfredson. 1980. *Decisionmaking in Criminal Justice: Toward the Rational Exercise of Discretion.* Cambridge, Mass.: Ballinger.

Gottfredson, M.R. & M.J. Hindelang. 1979a. "A study of 'The Behavior of Law'." *Amer.Sociol.Rev.*, 44:3–18.

———. 1979b. "Theory and research in the sociology of law." *Amer.Sociol.Rev.*, 44:27–36.

———. 1980. "Trite but true." *Amer.Sociol.Rev.*, 45:338–340.

Graham, H.D. & T.R. Gurr. 1969. *Violence in America: Historical and Comparative Perspectives: A Report to the National Commission on the Causes and Prevention of Violence.* Washington, D.C.: U.S. GPO.

Graves, W.F. 1964. "The deterrent effect of capital punishment in California." In H. Bedau (ed.), *The Death Penalty in America.* Garden City, N.Y.: Doubleday.

Green, E. 1964. "Inter- and intra-racial crime relative to sentencing." *Jour.Crim.Law, Crim., & Police Sci.*, 55:348–358.

Greenberg, D.F. 1975. "The incapacitative effect of imprisonment: Some estimates." *Law & Soc.Rev.*, 9:541–580.

Greenberg, D.F. et al 1979. "A panel model of crime rates and arrest rates." *Amer.Sociol.Rev.*, 44:843–850.

———. 1981. "Aggregation bias in deterrence research: An empirical analysis." *Jour.Res.Crime & Delinq.*, 18:128–137.

Griffiths, C.T. et al. 1980. *Criminal Justice in Canada: An Introductory Text.* Vancouver: Butterworth.

Guest, A.M. & J.J. Zuiches. 1977. "Another look at residential turnover in urban neighborhoods: A note on 'Racial change in a stable community' by Harvey Molotch," *Amer.Jour.Sociol.*, 77:457–467.

Gwaltney, J.L. 1980. *Drylongso.* New York: Random House.

Hacking, I. 1975. *The Emergence of Probability.* London: Cambridge University Press.

Hagan, J.L. 1974a. *Criminal Justice in a Canadian Province: A Study of the Sentencing Process.* Ph.D. dissertation. Edmonton: Department of Sociology, University of Alberta.

———. 1974b. "Extra-legal attributes and criminal sentencing: An assessment of a sociological viewpoint." *Law & Soc.Rev.*, 8:357–383.

———. 1975a. "The social and legal construction of criminal justice: A study of the pre-sentencing process." *Soc.Probs.*, 22:620–637.

———. 1975b. "Parameters of criminal prosecution: An application of path analysis to a problem of criminal justice." *Jour.Crim.Law & Crim.*, 65:536–544.

———. 1975c. "Law, order, and sentencing: A study of attitude in action." *Sociometry*, 38:374–384.

———. 1977b. "Finding 'discrimination': A question of meaning." *Ethnicity*, 4:167–176.

——. 1977c. *The Disreputable Pleasures*. Toronto: McGraw-Hill Ryerson.

Halatyn, T. 1975. *Violence Prediction Using Actuarial Methods: A Review and Prospectus*. Davis, Calif.: National Council on Crime and Delinquency Research Center.

Hall, E.T. 1959. *The Silent Language*. Garden City, N.Y.: Doubleday.

——. 1974. *Handbook for Proxemic Research*. Washington, D.C.: Society for the Anthropology of Visual Communication.

Hamparian, D.M. et al. 1978. *The Violent Few: A Study of Dangerous Juvenile Offenders*. Lexington, Mass.: Lexington Books.

Hann, R.G. et al. 1973. *Decision Making in the Canadian Criminal Court System: A Systems Analysis*. 2 vols. Toronto: Centre of Criminology, University of Toronto.

Harding, R.W. & R.P. Fahey. 1973. "Killings by Chicago police, 1969–1970: An empirical study." *So.Cal.Law Rev.*, 46:284–315.

Harland, A.T. 1981. *Restitution to Victims of Personal and Household Crimes*. Washington, D.C.: Bureau of Justice Statistics, U.S. Department of Justice.

Harvey, O.L. 1935. "The institutionalization of human sexual behavior: A study of frequency distributions." *Jour.Ab.Soc.Psych.*, 29:427–433.

Heath, A. 1976. *Rational Choice and Social Exchange: A critique of Exchange Theory*. Cambridge, Eng.: Cambridge U.P.

Herink, R. 1980. *The Psychotherapy Handbook*. New York: New American Library.

Hewett, F.M. 1965. "Teaching speech to an autistic child through operant conditioning." *Amer.Jour.Orthopsychiat.*, 35:927–936.

Hickey, J.E. & P.L. Scharf. 1980. *Toward a Just Correctional System: Experiments in Implementing Democracy in Prison*. San Francisco: Jossey-Bass.

Hoffman, C. & J.S. Reed. 1981. "Sex discrimination?—The XYZ affair." *Pub.Int.*, #62:21–39.

Hogarth, J. 1971. *Sentencing as a Human Process*. Toronto: Univ. Toronto Press.

Homans, G.C. 1961. *Social Behavior: Its Elementary Forms*. New York: Harcourt, Brace, World.

Hopkins, A. 1980. "Controlling corporate deviance." *Criminol.*, 18:198–214.

House Report. 1942. *Findings and Recommendations on Evacuation of Enemy Aliens and Others From Prohibited Military Zones*. Fourth Interim Report of the Select Committee Investigating National Defense Migration. House of Representatives. Washington, D.C.: U.S. GPO.

Howard, J. 1970. *Please Touch: A Guided Tour of the Human Potential Movement.* New York: McGraw-Hill.

Hudson, J. et al. 1977. "When criminals repay their victims: A survey of restitution programs." *Judicature,* 60:312–321.

Hundziak, M. et al. 1965. "Operant conditioning in toilet training of severely mentally retarded boys." *Amer.Jour.Mental Defic.,* 70:120–124.

Huxley, A. 1960. *Brave New World.* New York: Harper & Row.

Jacobson, D. et al. 1973. "A study of police referral of allegedly mentally-ill persons to a psychiatric unit." In J. Snibbe and H. Snibbe (eds.), *The Urban Policeman in Transition.* Springfield, Ill.: Thomas.

Janov, A. 1970. *The Primal Scream: Primal Therapy, the Cure for Neurosis.* New York: Putnam's Sons.

———. 1972. *The Primal Revolution: Toward a Real World.* New York: Simon & Schuster.

Jaspers, K. 1948. *Allgemeine Psychopathologie.* Berlin: Springer.

Johnson, E.H. 1957. "Selective factors in capital punishment." *Soc.Forces,* 36:165–169.

Johnson, G.B. 1941. "The Negro and crime." *Annals Amer.Acad. Pol.Soc.Sci.,* 277:93–104.

Judson, C.J. et al. 1969. "A study of the California penalty jury in first-degree-murder cases." *Stanford Law Rev.,* 21:1297–1497.

Kalven, H., Jr. & H. Zeisel. 1966. *The American Jury.* Boston: Little, Brown.

Kania, R.R.E. & W.C. Mackey. 1977. "Police violence as a function of community characteristics." *Crim.,* 15:27–48.

Kant, I. 1927. *Fundamental Principles of the Metaphysics of Morals.* Trans. by T.K. Abbott. London: Longmans, Green.

Kelsen, H. 1957. *What Is Justice?* Berkeley: Univ. Calif. Press.

Kennedy, W.A. 1965. "School phobia: Rapid treatment of fifty cases." *Jour.Ab.Psych.,* 70:285–289.

Kiesler, C.A. & M.S. Pallak. 1980. "The Virginia blues." *Amer.Psych.,* 35:953–954.

Kiev, A. 1968. *Psychiatry in the Communist World.* New York: Science House.

Klein, J.F. 1976. *Let's Make a Deal.* Lexington, Mass.: Lexington Books.

———. 1980. "Revitalizing restitution: Flogging a horse that may have been killed for just cause." In M.D. Schwartz et al (eds.), *Corrections: An Issues Approach.* Cincinnati: Anderson.

Klein, L.R. et al. 1978. "The deterrent effect of capital punishment: An assessment of the estimates." In A. Blumstein et al. (eds.), *Deterrence and Incapacitation: Estimating the Effects of Criminal Sanctions on Crime Rates.* Washington, D.C.: National Academy of Sciences.

Koch, S. 1974. "Psychology as science." In S.C. Brown (ed.), *Philosophy of Psychology.* London: Macmillan.

Konečni, V.J. and E.B. Ebbesen. 1982. "An analysis of the sentencing system." In V.J. Konečni and E.B. Ebbesen (eds.), *The Criminal Justice System: A Social-Psychological Analysis.* San Francisco: Freeman.

Koppin, M. 1976. *A Validation Study of Steadman's Legal Dangerousness Scale with Reference to Related Data.* Unpublished paper. Denver: Colorado State Hospital, Department of Research and Program Analysis.

Kozol, H.L., R.J. Boucher, and R.F. Garofalo. 1972. "The diagnosis and treatment of dangerousness." *Crime & Delinquency,* 18:371–392.

Krauss, L.I. & A. MacGahan. 1979. *Computer Fraud and Countermeasures.* Englewood Cliffs, N.J.: Prentice-Hall.

Kutner, L. 1968. "World outer space prison: A proposal." *Denver Law Rev.,* 45:702–781.

Ladd, J. 1957. *The Structure of a Moral Code.* Cambridge, Mass.: Harvard U.P.

LaFree, G.D. 1980. "The effect of sexual stratification by race on official reactions to rape." *Amer.Sociol.Rev.,* 45:842–854.

Lambley, P. 1981. *The Psychology of Apartheid.* London: Secker & Warburg.

Lancaster, H. & G.C. Hill. 1981. "Anatomy of a scam: Fraud at Wells Fargo depended on avoiding computer's red flags." *Wall St.Jour.,* 104:1, 20 (Feb. 26).

Landy, D. & E. Aronson. 1969. "The influence of the character of the criminal and his victim on the decisions of simulated jurors." *Jour.Exper.Soc.Psych.,* 5:141–152.

Lane, H.L. 1977. *The Wild Boy of Aveyron.* London: Allen & Unwin.

Langer, S. 1981. *"Scared Straight?": Fear in the Deterrence of Delinquency.* Washington, D.C.: University Press of America.

Law Enforcement Assistance Administration. 1979. "Computer crime at staggering level, fraud experts say." *Newsletter,* 9:3.

Law Reform Commission of Canada. 1974. *Restitution and Compensation.* Working Paper #5. Ottawa: Information Canada.

Levine, D.U. & J.K. Meyer. 1977. "Level and rate of desegregation and white enrollment decline in a big city school district." *Soc.Probs.*, 24:451–462.

Lindesmith, A.R. 1965. *The Addict and the Law.* Bloomington, Ind.: Indiana U.P.

Lindner, R.M. 1944. *Rebel Without a Cause: The Hypnoanalysis of a Criminal Psychopath.* New York: Grune & Stratton.

Lipton, D. et al. 1975. *The Effectiveness of Correctional Treatment: A Survey of Treatment Evaluation Studies.* New York: Praeger.

Livermore, J.M. et al. 1968. "On the justification for civil commitment." *Univ.Pa.Law Rev.,* 117:75–96.

Loftus, E.F. 1976. "Federal regulations: Make the punishment fit the crime." *Science,* 191:670 (Feb. 13).

Logan, C.H. 1972. "Evaluation research in crime and delinquency: A reappraisal." *Jour.Crim.Law, Crim., & Police Sci.,* 63:378–398.

Lovaas, O.I. et al 1965. "Experimental studies in childhood schizophrenia: Analysis of self-destructive behavior." *Jour.Exper.Child Psych.,* 2:67–84.

Lovibond, S.H. 1963. "The mechanism of conditioning treatment of enuresis." *Beh.Res. & Therapy,* 1:17–21.

Lundberg, G.A. & L. Dickson. 1952. "Inter-ethnic relations in a highschool population." *Amer.Jour.Sociol.,* 58:1–10.

Lundsgaarde, H.P. 1977. *Murder in Space City: A Cultural Analysis of Houston Homicide Patterns.* New York: Oxford U.P.

Lynn, R. 1961. "Introversion-extraversion differences in judgments of time." *Jour.Ab.Soc.Psych.,* 63:457–458.

MacKay, A.F. 1980. *Arrow's Theorem: The Paradox of Social Choice: A Case Study in the Philosophy of Economics.* New Haven: Yale U.P.

Malaparte, C. 1964. *The Skin.* Trans. by D. Moore. New York: Avon Books.

Massie. R.K. 1980. *Peter the Great: His Life and His World.* New York: Knopf.

McCauley, C. et al 1980. "Stereotyping: From prejudice to prediction." *Psych.Bull.,* 87:195–208.

McClintick, D. 1978. "Slow fade-out: At Columbia Pictures, a Hollywood scandal has lingering effects." *Wall St.Jour.,* 98:1, 12 (Jan. 30).

McConnell, J. 1970. "Stimulus/response: Criminals can be brainwashed—now." *Psych.Today,* 3:14–18, 74.

McCord, J. 1978. "A thirty-year follow-up of treatment effects." *Amer.Psych.,* 33:284–289.

———. 1980. "The treatment that did not help." *Soc.Action & Law,* 5:85–87.

McDowell, E. 1973. "Tending the spirit." *Wall St.Jour.,* 88:1, 11 (Mar. 26).

McNamara, H.P. 1975. *Newsletter.* Hackensack, N.J.: National Council on Crime and Delinquency.

Meehl, P.E. 1977. "Law and the fireside inductions: Some reflections of a clinical psychologist." In J.L. Tapp & F.G. Levine (eds.), *Law, Justice, and the Individual in Society: Psychological and Legal Issues.* New York: Holt, Rinehart, Winston.

Meehl, P.E. & A. Rosen. 1955. "Antecedent probability and the efficiency of psychometric signs." *Psych.Bull.,* 52:194–216.

Menninger, K.A. 1968. *The Crime of Punishment.* New York: Viking.

———. 1978. "Recollections of the dilemma about state hospitals in 1948, compared with the dilemma in corrections in 1977." *Bull. Amer.Aca. Psychiat. & Law,* 6:147–153.

Miller, T.I. 1981. "Consequences of restitution." *Law & Hum.Beh.,* 5:1–17.

Milton, S.H. et al. 1977. *Police Use of Deadly Force.* Washington, D.C.: The Police Foundation.

Minnesota Governor's Commission on Crime Prevention and Control. 1977. *Costs and Performance of Criminal Justice: A Statistical Analysis of Minnesota Counties.* St. Paul: Governor's Office.

Mitford, J. 1974. *Kind and Usual Punishment: The Prison Business.* New York: Vintage Books.

Molotch, H. 1969. "Racial integration in a transition community." *Amer.Sociol.Rev.,* 34:878–893.

Monahan, J. 1976. "Prediction research and the emergency commitment of dangerous mentally ill persons: A reconsideration." *Amer.Jour.Psychiat.,* 135:198–201.

———. 1978. "The prediction of violent criminal behavior: A methodological critique and prospectus." In A. Blumstein, J. Cohen, and D. Nagin (eds.), *Deterrence and Incapacitation: Estimating the Effects of Criminal Sanctions on Crime Rates.* Washington, D.C.: National Academy of Sciences.

———. 1980. *Who Is the Client?: The Ethics of Psychological Intervention in the Criminal Justice System.* Washington, D.C.: American Psychological Association.

Money, J. 1970. "Use of an androgen-depleting hormone in the treatment of male sex offenders." *Jour.Sex Res.,* 6:165–172.

Moore, R.J. 1980. *The Attitudes of Canadians Toward the Law and the Legal System.* Paper read at the annual meeting of the Law and Society Association. Madison, Wis. (June 6–9).

Morgan, P.M. 1977. *Deterrence: A Conceptual Analysis.* Beverly Hills: Sage.

Morris, N. 1977. "Who should go to prison?" In B.D. Sales (ed.), *Perspectives in Law and Psychology. I: The Criminal Justice System.* New York: Plenum.

Moss, H.A. & E.J. Susman. 1980. "Constancy and change in personality development." In O.G. Brim, Jr. & J. Kagan (eds.), *Constancy and Change in Human Development.* Cambridge, Mass.: Harvard U.P.

Moynihan, D.P. et al. 1965. *The Negro Family: The Case for National Action.* Washington, D.C.: U.S. GPO.

Murray, C.A. & L.A. Cox, Jr. 1979. *Beyond Probation: Juvenile Corrections and the Chronic Delinquent.* Beverly Hills: Sage.

Murray, C.A. et al. 1978. *UDIS: Deinstitutionalizing the Chronic Juvenile Offender.* Washington, D.C.: American Institutes for Research.

Myers, M.A. 1980a. "Predicting the behavior of law: A test for two models." *Law & Soc.Rev.,* 14:835–857.

———. 1980b. "Social contexts and attributions of criminal responsibility." *Soc.Psych.Quart.,* 43:405–419.

Nader, L. & H.F. Todd, Jr. 1978. *The Disputing Process: Law in Ten Societies.* New York: Columbia U.P.

Nagel, S.S. 1961. "Political party affiliation and judges' decisions." *Amer.Pol.Sci.Rev.,* 55:843–850.

———. 1965. *Disparities in Criminal Procedure.* Paper read at the annual meeting of the American Sociological Association.

Nagel, W.G. 1980. "Commentary." In C.H. Foust & D.R. Webster (eds.), *An Anatomy of Criminal Justice.* Lexington, Mass.: Lexington Books.

Nagin, D. 1978. "General deterrence: A review of the empirical evidence." In A. Blumstein et al. (eds.), *Deterrence and Incapacitation: Estimating the Effects of Criminal Sanctions on Crime Rates.* Washington, D.C.: National Academy of Sciences.

National Commission on the Causes and Prevention of Violence. 1969. *To Establish Justice, to Insure Domestic Tranquility: Final Report of the National Commission.* Washington, D.C.: U.S. GPO.

National Review. 1980a. "The week." 32:816 (July 11).

———. 1980b. "The week." 32:1304 (Nov. 14).

Nesbitt, W. & S. Candlish. 1978. "Determinism and the ability to do otherwise." *Mind,* 87:415–420.

Nettler, G. 1961. "Good men, bad men, and the perception of reality." *Sociometry,* 24:279–294.

———. 1976. *Social Concerns.* New York: McGraw-Hill.

——. 1979a. "Criminal justice." In A. Inkeles et al. (eds.), *Annual Review of Sociology*. Vol. 5. Palo Alto: Annual Reviews.

——. 1979b. *Responding to Crime: Radical Proposals.* Paper presented to the Centre for Criminology. Edmonton: University of Alberta (Feb. 15).

——. 1980. "Sociologist as advocate." *Can.Jour.Sociol.,* 5:31–53.

Newman, G. 1976. *Comparative Deviance: Perception and Law in Six Cultures.* New York: Elsevier.

Odiorne, G. 1963. "The trouble with sensitivity training." *Training & Develop.Jour.,* 3:9–20.

Ohio Legislative Service Commission. 1961. *Capital Punishment: Staff Research Report #46.* Columbus: The Commission.

Orwell, G. 1948, *Nineteen Eighty-Four.* New York: New American Library.

Outerbridge, W.R. 1968. "The tyranny of treatment ...?" *Can.Jour.Corrections.,* 10:378–387.

Padawer-Singer, A. & A.H. Barton. 1975. *Interim Report: Experimental Study of Decision Making in the 12-versus-6-Man Jury under Unanimous versus Non-unanimous Decisions.* New York: Bureau of Applied Social Research, Columbia University.

Palmer, T. 1978. *Correctional Intervention and Research.* Lexington, Mass.: Lexington Books.

Palumbo, D.R. 1977. *Statistics in Political and Behavioral Science.* 2nd ed. New York: Columbia U.P.

Parloff, M.B. 1979. "Can psychotherapy research guide the policymaker?: A little knowledge may be a dangerous thing." *Amer.Psych.,* 34:296–306.

Pateman, C. 1980. " 'The disorder of women': Women, love, and the sense of justice." *Ethics,* 91:20–34.

Patterson, G.R. et al 1965. "A behaviour modification technique for the hyperactive child." *Beh.Res. & Therapy,* 2:217–226.

——. 1973. "A social engineering technology for retraining the families of aggressive boys." In H.E. Adams & I.P. Unikel (eds.), *Issues and Trends in Behaviour Therapy.* Springfield, Ill.: Thomas.

Peck, J. 1976. "The deterrent effect of capital punishment." *Yale Law Jour.,* P6:359–367.

Penrod, S. & R. Hastie. 1979. "Models of jury decision making: A critical review." *Psych.Bull.,* 86:462–492.

Pepinsky, H.E. 1976. *Crime and Conflict: A Study of Law and Society.* New York: Academic Press.

Petersilia, J.R. & P.W. Greenwood. 1977. *Mandatory Prison Sentences: Their Projected Effects on Crime and Prison Populations.* Report P-6014. Santa Monica: Rand Corp.

Petersilia, et al. 1978. *Criminal Careers of Habitual Felons.* Report to the National Institute of Law Enforcement and Criminal Justice. Washington, D.C.: U.S. GPO.

Petersilia, J. & M. Lavin. 1978. *Targeting Career Criminals: A Developing Criminal Justice Strategy.* Santa Monica: Rand Corp.

Phillips, D.P. 1980. "The deterrent effect of capital punishment: New evidence on an old controversy." *Amer.Jour.Sociol.,* 86:139–148.

Piasecki, J. 1975. *Community Response to Residential Services for the Psychosocially Disabled: Preliminary Results of a National Survey.* Paper read at the First Annual Conference of the International Association of Psycho-Social Rehabilitation Services. Philadelphia.

Piel, G. 1961. *Consumers of Abundance.* Occasional Papers of the Center for the Study of Democratic Institutions. Santa Barbara: The Center.

Pilot Alberta Restitution Centre. 1976. *Progress Report: September 1, 1975–November 30, 1976.* Calgary: The Centre.

Pokorny, A.D. 1965. "A comparison of homicides in two cities." *Jour.Crim.Law, Crim., & Police Sci.,* 56:479–487.

Pontell, H.N. 1978. "Deterrence: Theory versus practice." *Crim.,* 16:3–22.

Posner, R.A. 1980. "Retribution and related concepts of punishment." *Jour.Legal Studies,* 9:71–92.

Press, S.J. 1977. "Police manpower versus crime." In J.M. Tanur et al. (eds.), *Statistics: A Guide to Political and Social Issues.* San Francisco: Holden-Day.

Rabkin, J.G. 1979. "Criminal behavior of discharged mental patients: A critical appraisal of the research." *Psych.Bull.,* 86:1–27.

Rachman, S.J. & G.T. Wilson 1980. *The Effects of Psychological Therapy.* 2nd ed. Oxford: Pergamon.

Radzinowicz, L. & J. King. 1977. *The Growth of Crime: The International Experience.* London: Hamish Hamilton.

Rahav, G. 1980. "Ethnic origins and the disposition of delinquents in Israel." *Inter.Jour.Comp. & Appl. Crim.Justice,* 4:63–74.

Rainwater, L. & W.L. Yancey. 1967. *The Moynihan Report and the Politics of Controversy.* Cambridge, Mass.: MIT Press.

Ramsey, S.J. 1976. "Prison codes." *Jour.Communic.,* 26:39–45.

Rapoport, A. 1950. *Science and the Goals of Man: A Study in Semantic Orientation.* New York: Harper.

Rector, M.H. 1977. *Should We Build More Prisons?* Hackensack, N.J.: National Council on Crime & Delinquency.

Reed, J.P. & R.S. Reed. 1977. "Liberalism-conservatism as an indicator of jury product and process." *Law & Hum.Beh.,* 1:81–86.

Reed. T.E. 1977. "Racial comparisons of alcohol metabolism: Background problems and results." *Alcoholism: Clin.Exper.Res.,* 2:83–87.

Reich, W. 1973. *The Function of the Orgasm: Sex-Economic Problems of Biological Energy.* New York: Farrar, Straus, Giroux.

Rettig, S. & B. Pasamanick. 1964. "Differential judgment of ethical risk by cheaters and noncheaters." *Jour.Ab.Soc.Psych.,* 69:109–113.

Rife, D.C. 1948. "Genetic variability within a student population." *Amer.Jour.Phys.Anthro.,* 6:47–62.

Robins, L.N. & S.Y. Hill. 1966. "Assessing the contributions of family structure, class, and peer groups in juvenile delinquency." *Jour.Crim. Law, Crim., & Police Sci.,* 57:325–334.

Robison, J. 1969. *It's Time to Stop Counting: The California Prison, Parole, and Probation System.* Technical Supplement #2, A Special Report to the Assembly. Sacramento: Legislative Assembly.

Roof, W.C. 1972. "Residential segregation of blacks and racial inequality in southern cities: Toward a causal model." *Soc.Probs.,* 19:393–407.

Roof, W.C. et al. 1976. "Residential segregation in Southern cities: 1970." *Soc.Forces,* 55:59–71.

Roper, R.T. 1980. "Jury size and verdict consistency: A line has to be drawn somewhere?" *Law & Soc.Rev.,* 14:977–999.

Ross, H.L. 1977. "Deterrence regained: The Cheshire constabulary's 'breathalyser blitz'."

Ross, H.L. et al. 1970. "Determining the social effects of a legal reform: The British 'breathalyser' crackdown of 1967." *Amer.Beh.Sci.,* 13:493–509.

Ross, Ian. 1981. *Medicolegal Categories of Death: Taxonomic Problems.* Ph.D. dissertation. Edmonton: Department of Sociology, University of Alberta.

Ross, R.R. 1975. *The Effectiveness of Behavioural Treatment Programs for Female Delinquents in a Correctional Institution.* Paper read at the Symposium on New Trends in Criminology.

Ross, R.R. & P. Gendreau (eds.). 1980. *Effective Correctional Treatment.* Toronto: Butterworths.

Ross, R.R. & H.B. McKay. 1976. "A study of institutional treatment programs." *Internat.Jour.Offender Therapy & Compar.Crim.,* 20:165–173.

Rossell, C.H. et al. 1978. "Busing and 'white flight'." *Pub.Int.,* #53:109–115.

Rowan, R. 1980. "ABC covers itself." *Fortune,* 102:45–48 (Nov. 17).

Rozelle, R.M. & J.C. Baxter. 1975. "Impression formation and danger recognition in experienced police officers." *Jour.Soc.Psych.,* 96:53–63.

Russell, F. 1975. *A City in Terror.* New York: Viking.

Russell, J.C. 1979. "Perceived action units as a function of subjective importance." *Person.Soc.Psych.Bull.,* 5:206–209.

Rutter, M. et al. 1964. "Temperamental characteristics in infancy and the later development of behavioural disorders." *Br.Jour.Psychiat.,* 110·651–661.

Sagarin, A. & A. Karmen. 1978. "Criminology and the reaffirmation of humanist ideals." *Crim.,* 16:239–254.

Salem, R.G. & W.J. Bowers. 1970. "Severity of formal sanctions as a deterrent to deviant behavior." *Law & Soc.Rev.,* 5:21–40.

Salili, F. et al. 1976. "Achievement and morality: A cross-cultural analysis of causal attribution and evaluation." *Jour.Person.Soc.Psych.,* 33:327–337.

Sanders, C.R. 1975. "Caught in the con game: The young, white drug user's contact with the legal system." *Law & Soc.Rev.,* 9:197–218.

Sargant, W. 1964. "Psychiatric treatment: Here and there." *Atlantic Monthly,* 214:88–95.

Savitz, L. 1958. "A study in capital punishment." *Jour.Crim.Law, Crim., & Police Sci.,* 49:338–341.

Schellhardt, T.R. 1978. "Revising the U.S. criminal code." *Wall St.Jour.,* 98:14 (June 16).

Scherman, K. 1972. "Iceland." Foreword to R. Roberts et al., *Fisher/ Spassky: The New York Times Report on the Chess Match of the Century.* New York: Quadrangle.

Schwendinger, H. & J. Schwendinger. 1975. "Defenders of order or guardians of human rights?" In I. Taylor et al. (eds.), *Critical Criminology.* London: Routledge & Kegan Paul.

Sechrest, L. et al. 1979. *Rehabilitation of Criminal Offenders: Problems and Prospects.* Washington, D.C.: National Academy of Sciences.

Seligman, D. 1978c. "Numbers game." *Fortune,* 98:36 (Dec. 4).

——. 1980a. "A score for the crooks." *Fortune,* 102:45–46 (June 30).

——. 1980b. "Masochism in accounting." *Fortune,* 102:42 (Nov. 3).

Sellin, T. 1959. *The Death Penalty.* Philadelphia: The American Law Institute.

——. 1961. "Capital punishment." *Fed.Prob.,* 25:3–11.

Shack, B. 1980. Cited by N. Maxwell, "Words whispered to subconscious supposedly deter thefts, fainting." *Wall St.Jour.*, 103:25 (Nov. 25).

Shaplen, R. 1978. "Annals of crime: The Lockheed incident." *The New Yorker*, 53:48–74 (Jan. 23).

Sharp, F. & M. Otto. 1910. "A study of the popular attitude toward retributive punishment." *Internat.Jour.Ethics*, 20:341–357.

Shea, M.A. 1974. "A study of the effect of the prosecutor's choice of charge on magistrate's sentencing behaviour." *Br.Jour.Crim.*, 14:269–272.

Shinnar, R. & S. Shinnar. 1975. "The effects of the criminal justice system on the control of crime: A quantitative approach." *Law & Soc.Rev.*, 9:581–611.

Silberman, C.E. 1978. *Criminal Violence, Criminal Justice.* New York: Random House.

Simmel, G. 1950. *The Sociology of Georg Simmel.* Trans. by K.H. Wolff. New York: Free Press.

Simon, C.K. 1978. "Crime—What punishment?" *Freedom at Issue*, #48:22–25.

Smart, C. 1976. *Women, Crime, and Criminology: A Feminist Critique.* London: Routledge & Kegan Paul.

Smith, K.J. 1965. *A Cure for Crime: The Case for the Self-determinate Sentence.* London: Duckworth.

Smith, L. 1978. " 'Equal opportunity' rules are getting tougher." *Fortune*, 97:152–156 (June 19).

Smith, M. 1966. "Percy Foreman: Top trial lawyer." *Life*, 60:91–101.

Snare, F.E. 1980. "The diversity of morals." *Mind*, 89:353–369.

Solicitor General, Alberta. 1978. "People may think I'm soft—Farran." *Edmonton Journal*, p. B-4 (Nov. 9).

Solicitor General, Canada. 1975. *Young Persons in Conflict with the Law: A Report on Proposals for New Legislation to Replace the Juvenile Delinquents Act.* Ottawa: Ministry of the Solicitor General.

Sommer, R. 1969. *Personal Space: The Behavioral Basis of Design.* Englewood Cliffs, N.J.: Prentice-Hall.

———. 1976. *The End of Imprisonment.* New York: Oxford U.P.

Sonnenfeld, J. & P.L. Lawrence. 1978. "Why do companies succumb to price fixing?" *Harvard Bus.Rev.*, 56:145–157.

Sowell, T. 1978. "Are quotas good for blacks?" *Commentary*, 65:39–43.

Stafford, J. 1973. "Touch and go." *New York Rev.Books*, 20:30–33 (Apr. 5).

Staub, H. & F.G. Alexander. 1962. *The Criminal, the Judge, and the Public: A Psychological Analysis.* New York: Collier.

Steadman, H.J. 1973. "Some evidence on the inadequacy of the concept and determination of dangerousness in law and psychiatry." *Jour.Psychiat. & Law,* 1:409–426.

Steadman, H.J. and J.J. Cocozza. 1974. *Careers of the Criminally Insane.* Lexington, Ma.: Lexington Books.

Stephan, C. & J.C. Tully. 1977. "The influence of physical attractiveness of a plaintiff on the decisions of simulated jurors." *Jour.Soc.Psych.,* 101:149–150.

Sterling, C. 1978. "The terrorist network." *Atlantic Monthly,* 242:37–47.

Stern, P.J. 1972. *In Praise of Madness: Realness Therapy—The Self Reclaimed.* New York: Norton.

Stigler, G.J. 1970. "The optimum enforcement of laws." *Jour.Pol.Econ.,* 78:526–536.

Strawson, P.F. 1981. "Doers and their doings." *Times Lit.Suppl.,* #4062:127–128 (Feb. 6).

Strong, E.K., Jr. 1962. "Nineteen year follow-up of engineer interests." *Jour.Appl.Psych.,* 36:65–74.

Sutherland, S. 1980. "The profession of care." *Times Lit.Suppl.,* #4052:1347 (Nov. 28).

Swanson, C.R. & L. Territo. 1980. "Computer crime: Dimensions, types, causes, and investigation." *Jour.Police Sci.Admin.,* 8:304–311.

Szasz, T.S. 1957. "Commitment of the mentally ill: 'Treatment' or social restraint?" *Jour.Nerv.Mental Dis.,* 125:293.

———. 1958. "Politics and mental health: Some remarks apropos of the case of Mr. Ezra Pound." *Amer.Jour.Psychiat.,* 115:508.

———. 1963. *Law, Liberty, and Psychiatry: An Inquiry into the Social Use of Mental Health Practices.* New York: Macmillan.

Tanay, E. 1979. "The Baxstrom affair and psychiatry." *Jour.Forensic Scis.,* 24:663–672.

Tate, B.G. & G.S. Baroff. 1966. "Aversive control of self-injurious behavior in a psychotic boy." *Beh.Res. & Therapy,* 4:281–287.

Taylor, R. 1967. "Causation." In P. Edwards (ed.), *The Encyclopedia of Philosophy.* New York: Macmillan.

Tedrow, R.L. & T.I. Tedrow. 1976. *Death at Chappaquiddick.* Ottawa, Ill.: Caroline House.

Teevan, J.J., Jr. 1972. "Deterrent effects of punishment: The Canadian case." *Can.Jour.Corrections,* 14:68–82.

Thomas, A. et al. 1970. "The origin of personality." *Sci.Amer.,* 223:102–109.

Thomson, R.J. & M.T. Zingraff. 1981. "Detecting sentencing disparity: Some problems and evidence." *Amer.Jour.Sociol.,* 86:869–880.

Tifft, L. & D. Sullivan. 1980. *The Struggle to Be Human: Crime, Criminology, and Anarchism.* Mt. Pleasant, Mich.: Cienfuegos Press.

Tittle, C.R. & C.H. Logan. 1973. "Sanctions and deviance: Evidence and the remaining questions." *Law & Soc.Rev.,* 7:371–392.

Toch, H. 1969. *Violent Men.* Chicago: Aldine.

Totaro, R. 1978. Cited by *National Review,* "The week." 30:1458 (Nov. 24).

Tufte, E.R. 1974. *Data Analysis for Politics and Policy.* Englewood Cliffs, N.J.: Prentice-Hall.

Tussman, J. 1977. *Government and the Mind.* New York: Oxford U.P.

Tversky, A. and D. Kahneman. 1980. "Causal schemas in judgment under uncertainty." In M. Fishbein (ed.), *Progress in Social Psychology.* Hillsdale, N.J.: Erlbaum.

———. 1981. "The framing of decisions and the psychology of choice." *Science,* 211:453–458 (Jan. 30).

Uhlman, T.M. & N.D. Walker. 1980. " 'He takes some of my time; I take some of his': An analysis of judicial sentencing patterns in jury cases." *Law & Soc.Rev.,* 14:323–341.

Underwood, W.J. 1965. "Evaluation of laboratory method training." *Training Director's Jour.,* 19:34–40.

United Press International. 1980d. "Castration rejected for convicted rapist." (Jan. 10).

United States Commission. 1969. *National Commission on the Causes and Prevention of Violence.* Staff Reports, 13 volumes. Washington, D.C.: U.S. GPO.

United States Commission on Obscenity and Pornography. 1970. *The Report of the Commission on Obscenity and Pornography.* Washington, D.C.: U.S. GPO.

United States v. Charnizon. 1967. Washington, D.C.: Municipal Court of Appeals, 232:586.

U.S. Department of Justice. 1974. *Crime in Eight American Cities.* Washington, D.C.: U.S. GPO.

U.S. News & World Report. 1978. "Weeding out clergymen who go astray." 85:63–65 (Oct. 2).

Van Dine St. et al. 1979. *Restraining the Wicked: The Incapacitation of the Dangerous Criminal.* Lexington, Mass.: Lexington Books.

Van Valey, T.L. et al. 1977. "Trends in residential segregation, 1960–1970." *Amer.Jour.Sociol.,* 82:826–844.

Vidmar, N. 1974. "Retributive and utilitarian motives and other correlates of Canadian attitudes toward the death penalty." *Can.Psych.,*
15:337–356.

Vidmar, N. & L. Crinklaw. 1973. *Retribution and Utility as Motives in
Sanctioning Behavior.* Paper read at the annual meeting of the Midwestern Psychological Association. Chicago.

Vidmar, N. & P. Ellsworth. 1974. "Public opinion and the death penalty." *Stanford Law Rev.,* 26:1245–1270.

Vidmar, N. & D.T. Miller 1980. "Socio-psychological processes under-
lying attitudes toward legal punishment." *Law & Soc.Rev.,*
14:565–602.

von Mises, R. 1957. *Probability, Statistics, and Truth.* London: George
Allen & Unwin.

Walker, T.G. 1972. "A note concerning partisan influences on trial
judge decision making." *Law & Soc.Rev.,* 6:645–650.

Wall Street Journal. 1980e. "Laundered cash payments didn't soil this
tax return." 102:1 (Apr. 23).

Ward, D.A. et al. 1969. "Crimes of violence by women." In D.
Mulvihill et al. (eds.), *Crimes of Violence.* Vol. 13. Washington,
D.C.: U.S. GPO.

Warriner, C.K. 1958. "The nature and functions of official morality."
Amer.Jour.Sociol., 64:165–168.

Watt, R.M. 1963. *Dare Call It Treason.* New York: Simon & Schuster.

Wechsler, J.A. et al. 1972. *In a Darkness.* New York: Norton.

Weinberg, T.S. 1978. "Sadism and masochism : Sociological perspectives." *Bull. Amer.Aca. Psychiat. & Law,* 6:284–295.

Weinstein, L. 1964. "Real and ideal discharge criteria." *Mental Hospitals,* 15:680–683.

Wenk, E.A. and R.L. Emrich. 1972. "Assaultive youth: An exploratory
study of the assaultive experience and assaultive potential of California Youth Authority wards." *Journal of Research in Crime and
Delinquency,* 9:171–196.

Wenk, E.A., J.O. Robison, and G.W. Smith. 1972. "Can violence be
predicted?" *Crime & Delinquency,* 18:393–402.

Wexler, S. 1975. "Discretion: The unacknowledged side of law."
Univ.Toronto Law Jour., 25:120–182.

Wheeler, S. et al. 1968. "Agents of delinquency control: A comparative analysis." In S. Wheeler (ed.), *Controlling Delinquents.*
New York: Wiley.

Wildavsky, A. 1979. *Speaking Truth to Power: The Art and Craft of
Policy Analysis.* Toronto: Little. Brown.

Wilkins, R. 1981. "The widening social chasm." *Fortune,* 103:115 (Mar. 9).

Willcock, H.D. 1974. *Deterrents and Incentives to Crime Among Boys and Young Men Aged 15 to 21 Years.* London: Office of Population Censuses and Surveys.

Wilson, J.Q. 1968. "The police and the delinquent in two cities." In S. Wheeler (ed.), *Controlling Delinquents.* New York: Wiley.

Wilson, J.Q. & B. Boland. 1976. "Crime." In W. Gorham & N. Glazer (eds.), *The Urban Predicament.* Washington, D.C.: The Urban Institute.

Wilson, J.Q. & B. Boland. 1978. "The effect of the police on crime." *Law & Soc.Rev.,* 12:367–390.

Wilson, R.S. 1974. "Twins: Mental development in the pre-school years." *Develop. Psych.,* 10:580–588.

——. 1978. "Synchronies in mental development: An epigenetic perspective." *Science,* 202:939–948 (Dec. 1).

Wittgenstein, L. 1922. *Tractatus Logico-Philosophicus.* New York: Harcourt, Brace.

Wolf, L. 1974. "Surrogate wives: A closer look at the new professionals." *Playgirl,* 1:24–55, 136.

Wolfgang, M.E. 1974. "The social scientist in court." *Jour.Crim. Law & Crim.,* 65:239–247.

Wolfgang, M.E. & J.J. Collins, Jr. 1977. *Offender Careers and Restraint: Probabilities and Policy Implications.* Washington, D.C.: National Institute of Juvenile Justice & Delinquency Prevention.

Wolfgang, M.E. et al. 1972. *Delinquency in a Birth Cohort.* Chicago: Univ. Chicago Press.

Wolfgang, M.E. & M. Riedel. 1973. "Race, judicial discretion, and the death penalty." *Annals Amer.Aca.Pol.Soc.Sci.,* 407:119–133.

——. 1976. "Rape, racial discrimination, and the death penalty." In H.A. Bedau & C.M. Pierce (eds.), *Capital Punishment in the United States.* New York: AMS Press.

——. 1977. "Race, rape, and the death penalty." In D. Chappell et al. (eds.), *Forcible Rape: The Crime, the Victim, and the Offender.* New York: Columbia U.P.

Wolpe, J. 1981. "Behavior therapy versus psychoanalysis." *Amer.Psych.,* 36:159–164.

Wootton, B. 1978. *Crime and Penal Policy: Reflections of Fifty Years' Experience.* London: Allen & Unwin.

Wortis, J. 1950. *Soviet Psychiatry.* Baltimore: Williams & Wilkins.

Yolton, J. 1973. "Action: Metaphysic and modality." *Amer.Phil.Quart.,* 10:71–85.

Zahn, M. 1974. *Death by Murder: A Comparison Between Female Drug Users and Female Non-Users.* Paper read at the annual meeting of the Society for the Study of Social Problems. Montreal.

Zimring, F.E. et al. 1976. "Punishing homicide in Philadelphia: Perspectives on the death penalty." *Univ.Chicago Law Rev.,* 43:227–252.

Zimring, F.E. & G.J. Hawkins. 1973. *Deterrence: The Legal Threat in Crime Control.* Chicago: Univ. Chicago Press.

Zinn, H. 1967. "History as private enterprise." In K.H. Wolff & B. Moore (eds.), *The Critical Spirit.* Boston: Beacon Press.

NAME INDEX

SUBJECT INDEX

Rate, refined, 87, 98
Rationality:
  and diversity, 6
  knowing what one is doing, 2, 9, 95
  and morality, 2, 62, 63, 67, 150
Reasons:
  not causes, 2, 95
  for responding to crime, 5–6
Rehabilitation (*see* Corrections, Therapies)
Reprobation:
  defined, 13
  and moral education, 9
Research requirements, 32–36, 45–46
Restitution:
  defined, 17
  as sentence, 18–19
  as therapy, 17, 20–21
  not victim-compensation, 17
Retribution:
  as "crime," 16
  defined, 9
  and moral distance, 14–15
  morality of, 12–13
  not revenge, 11, 13
  utility of, 12–13
Rules, 112

Safety crimes, 69
Science, 16
Selection ratio, 83, 84
Sensitivity, test, 84
Social choice (*see also* Policy):
  and knowledge, 121–122
  paradox of, 3–5
Social engineering, 141, 142
Social work, 94, 131
Specificity, test, 84
State, 26
Stereotypy, 97

Talion, law of, 12
Target hardening, 141–143